W9-ANK-593

Sandusky

Sandusky

by

Linda C. Ashar

Sandusky (*Tourist Town Guides*®)
© 2010 by Linda C. Ashar

Published by:
Channel Lake, Inc., P.O. Box 1771, New York, NY 10156-1771
http://www.channellake.com

Author: Linda C. Ashar
Editorial and Page Layout: Quadrum Solutions (http://www.quadrumltd.com)
Cover Design: Julianna Lee
Front Cover Photos:
"Marblehead Lighthouse" © stock.xchng/Toby Boyce
"Cedar Point" © stock.xchng
"Boy with the Boot" © Linda C. Ashar
Back Cover Photo:
"Follett House" © Linda C. Ashar

Published in May, 2010

ISBN-13: 978-0-9767064-5-8

Disclaimer: The information in this book has been checked for accuracy. However, neither the publisher nor the author may be held liable for errors or omissions. *Use this book at your own risk.* To obtain the latest information, we recommend that you contact the vendors directly. If you do find an error, let us know at corrections@channellake.com

Channel Lake, Inc. is not affiliated with the vendors mentioned in this book, and the vendors have not authorized, approved or endorsed the information contained herein. This book contains the opinions of the author, and your experience may vary.

For more information, visit http://www.touristtown.com

Help Our Environment!

Even when on vacation, your responsibility to protect the environment does not end. Here are some ways you can help our planet without spoiling your fun:

★ Ask your hotel staff not to clean your towels and bed linens each day. This reduces water waste and detergent pollution.

★ Turn off the lights, heater, and/or air conditioner when you leave your hotel room.

★ Use public transportation when available. Tourist trolleys are very popular, and they are usually cheaper and easier than a car.

★ Recycle everything you can, and properly dispose of rubbish in labeled receptacles.

Tourist towns consume a lot of energy. Have fun, but don't be wasteful. Please do your part to ensure that these attractions are around for future generations to visit and enjoy.

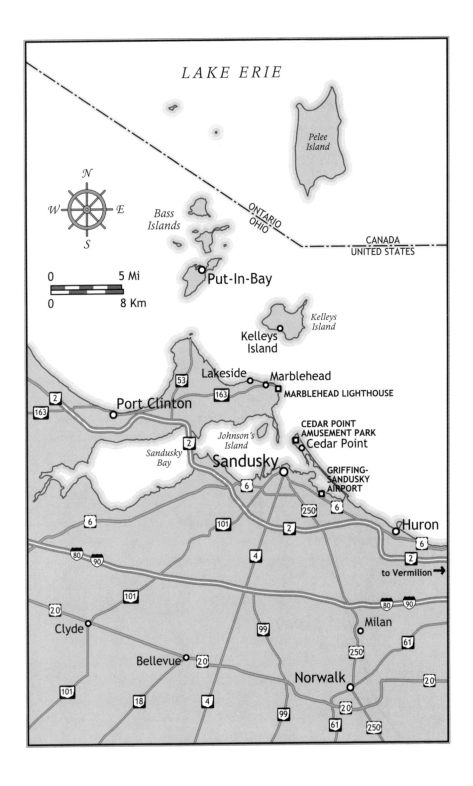

Dedicated to my mother,
Genevieve Mae Smith Clark

Cedar Point Amusement Park,
which began its mission to
entertain well over 100 years ago,
has not stopped since.

Table of Contents

How to Use this Book

Tourist Town Guides® makes it easy to find exactly what you are looking for! Just flip to a chapter or section that interests you. The tabs on the margins will help you find your way quickly.

Attractions are usually listed by subject groups. Attractions may have an address, Web site (●), and/or telephone number (☎) listed.

Must-See Attractions: Headlining must-see attractions, or those that are otherwise iconic or defining, are designated with the ✪ **Must See!** symbol.

Coverage: This book is not all-inclusive. It is comprehensive, with many different options for entertainment, dining, shopping, etc. but there are many establishments not listed here.

Pricing is not provided; some places are free, but may not remain so in the future. Pricing for many places changes between "in season" and "off season" and therefore cannot be accurately represented. Pricing also changes from year to year. Many places offer discounts and "package deals" or coupon specials. For these reasons it is impossible to predict or rate the cost of attractions with accuracy. The best planning for expenses for the attractions is to check specific places of interest at the time of visit. Many list their rates online for various times of the year and for special package deals.

A key to enjoying Cedar Point's many attractions is planning in advance to take maximum advantage of available discounts.

Introduction

There is an irresistible – almost mystical – aura around the land, the rivers, and waters of Lake Erie and the wildlife that inhabit them. People come to the area to seek their fortune, make new beginnings, and find a retreat to rest and restore their health and escape the routine of daily life. People seeking their personal visions may or may not find them here, but they continue to come every year.

More than anything else, these days visitors come to the Sandusky area for recreation and relaxation. One dominating attraction of this playground on Ohio's North Coast is the grand **Cedar Point Amusement Park**, which began its mission to entertain well over 100 years ago and has not stopped since. Attractions of every sort have sprung up along the lake, some old, others always new, seeking to capture the public's attention in the tourist economy.

Other permanent mainstays of the area are the islands – Put-in-Bay (South Bass Island), Middle Bass Island, Kelleys Island – and the Catawba and Marblehead Peninsulas. In the center of it all stands Sandusky, recently named by *The New Rating Guide to Life in America's Small Cities* as America's 6th Best Small City.

This book offers an independent guide and historical retrospective of the area. Perhaps it will pique your interest and provide a variety of things to see and do, places to visit, and accommodations to stay in. It is *not* intended to be all-inclusive. The fact that a place is omitted or not marked "must-see" should not be inferred to be a negative commentary. Also, places and attractions are constantly in a state of flux. Be aware that life is fluid and things change. Always check in advance when planning your visits to confirm the most up-to-date information.

Some of the attractions and places mention that they are family friendly. This, however, may not meet the requirements of all families. Readers are encouraged to contact each place of interest for specific information, not just for times and prices, but for facts about its amenities and services that may be important for specific comfort, needs, and accessibility.

AREA ORIENTATION

Sandusky is located on Ohio's North Coast on Lake Erie, sheltered by Sandusky Bay. Being near the Ohio Turnpike I-80 and State Rt. 2, Sandusky and its environs are conveniently accessible by car: approximately one hour from Cleveland, Ohio; two hours from Detroit, Michigan; 2.5 hours from Columbus, Ohio; one hour from Toledo, Ohio; 3.5 hours from Pittsburgh, Pennsylvania; and 4.5 hours from Chicago, Illinois.

GETTING TO SANDUSKY

The closest large commercial airports are located in Cleveland, Toledo, and Detroit. Private or local airports for smaller aircraft are Griffing Flying Service in Sandusky, Norwalk-Huron County Airport in nearby Norwalk, Port Clinton, and Fremont. South Bass Island and Kelleys Island also have airstrips.

For those journeying to Sandusky by train, **Amtrak** (☎ 800.872.7245 ◗ amtrak.com) has an unmanned stop at 1200 N. Depot St. in Sandusky. There is no ticket office or any other service at this station.

Greyhound bus is located at 6513 Milan Rd., U.S. Route 250, Sandusky (☎ *419.625.6907 or 800.454.2487 ● greyhound.com*).

For those who wish to come here by private boat, there are many private and public access marinas and boat and yacht clubs with reciprocal membership privileges. Sandusky has a municipal boat ramp. Off the mainland, within easy ferry or air commute, are the Lake Erie Islands, most notably South Bass Island, home to "party central" Put-in-Bay, and Kelleys Island, another favorite watering hole and vacation spot. More laidback is Middle Bass Island. Farther out is Canada's Peelee Island.

Dockage can also be found along the coastline in nearby towns from Cleveland to Toledo. Located east of Sandusky and along the shore are Huron and Vermilion, while west are Port Clinton, Catawba, Marblehead, and Lakeside.

Milan, Norwalk, Fremont, and Bellevue are situated just a bit south/southwest. All these areas, with their history, marinas, nature preserves, fishing, shopping, sights, restaurants, and entertainment, seamlessly weave their attractions into Sandusky's Ohio playground.

SANDUSKY ATTRACTIONS

Famous as a tourist playground because of the many attractions such as those headlined by **Cedar Point Amusement Park**, the Sandusky area is equally notable for its many nature reserves, a rich resource for the study of delicate ecosystems, fish, waterfowl, and other wildlife. The area shelters the American bald eagle and other endangered species. Sandusky is a home base for the Ohio Department of Natural Resources' Coastal Management Program. This is one of only 34 such programs nationwide that have been approved and funded by the National Oceanic and Atmospheric Administration (NOAA).

Fishing and boating, expected pursuits on an inland sea, are especially attractive in this area due to the relatively protected harbor provided by Sandusky Bay. Divers interested in submerged shipwrecks have many opportunities for underwater discovery in the western Lake Erie basin.

The Sandusky area has also been a notable crossroads in history, right from Paleolithic times up to the settlement of the United States. The **Glacial Grooves** on Kelleys Island testify to the receding glacier of the Ice Age; the transition of native tribes on the land has been recorded through study of artifacts displayed in various study venues, such as the **Old Woman's Creek Visitors Center** in Huron and on Kelleys Island. The numerous rivers of Ohio's northern watershed, the Great Lakes, and native trails brought settlers out to this natural place for fostering trade, industry, travel, and communication. Sandusky remains at the heart of these places of interest.

TRANSPORTATION

The area is best explored by car and by boat for the shore island adventures. Ferry and air services are available on regular schedules in the summer seasons to Put-in-Bay, Middle Bass, and Kelleys Island. During off-season periods, it is more of a hit-or-miss situation, depending on the weather.

A GPS system is always useful. For Sandusky, a city map in hand will be helpful as well, for Sandusky was not laid out on a traditional parallel street grid. The city was designed upon the Masonic emblem, making for a more complex street system.

Ultimately, of course, sightseeing and playing will be on foot. Most of the best places to see are handicap accessible. Traveling the region can be done by air, road, or by boat. All three are convenient options for tourists visiting the area.

GETTING AROUND BY FERRY

Tourists interested in traversing the Islands by water can hop on board any of the several ferries that ply the waters.

MILLER FERRY

(● millerferry.com) Based in Put-in-Bay on South Bass Island, Miller Ferry's mainland dock is located at the tip of Route 54, northwest of Sandusky. The ferry accommodates vehicles, including RVs, trailers, and boats, and makes stops on its circuit at Put-in-Bay (South Bass Island) and Middle Bass Island. It runs on a regular schedule during the summer season but the weather dictates the ferry schedule during the off-season. Miller Ferry's Web site provides good current information of the ferry schedule, fare rates, and a wealth of other travel information. Fares are reasonable. Like many area businesses, Miller Ferry is family operated. Its motto is to take care of its customers, safety first.

JET EXPRESS

(● jet-express.com) The Jet Express is an attraction in and of itself. The Jet is a catamaran fleet that seems to "fly" as it skims over the top of the water. The Jet boats provide comfortable seating inside and tiered outdoor decks. It provides service to Put-in-Bay and Kelleys Island from downtown Sandusky's

Jackson Street Pier and to Put-in-Bay from its port at #3 North Monroe Street in Port Clinton. It also offers inter-island hopping service between Put-in-Bay and Kelleys Island. The Jet Express does not operate during the winter season. Check the Web site for schedules and rates. Tickets to Put-in-Bay can be purchased online. The Jet accommodates people only, not vehicles, and is pricier than some of the other ferry services.

KELLEYS ISLAND FERRY

(510 West Main St., Route 163, Marblehead
kelleyislandferry.com) The Kelleys Island Ferry operates year-round, with its schedule subject to weather and ice conditions on a day-to-day basis in the winter season. It runs from its dock out of Marblehead. The Kelleys Island Ferry can accommodate most vehicles, including tractor trailers, RVs, horse trailers, and boats. Passengers can stay in their vehicles or go inside for the comfort of the ferry lounge during their trip across. Group discounts are available. Check the Web site for the ferry schedule, especially during the winter season. All trips are always dependent on the weather and the ferry office remains closed on Christmas Day.

GETTING AROUND BY AIR

Apart from flying into Sandusky, tourists can avail of charters that provide them the option of viewing the beauty of the region from high up in the air.

DAIRY AIR

(☎ 800.647.0837) Based on South Bass Island, Dairy Air operates between Put-In-Bay and Fremont's local airport near Sandusky. The flight takes about 15 minutes. If your pilot is in the mood, you may even get a shoreline air tour thrown in for fun.

GRIFFING FLYING SERVICES AIRPORT

(🖱 griffingflyingservice.com) Closest to Sandusky and Cedar Point, Griffing offers charter services, Canada service, customs, island flights, and scenic tours. There is a shuttle service to Cedar Point for those who fly in for a day or for a stay at the amusement park (landing and parking fees apply). Call for flight reservations. Information about rates, car rental, and customs service is kept up-to-date on Griffing's Web site.

ERIE OTTAWA REGIONAL AIRPORT

(🖱 portclintonairport.com) Erie Ottawa Regional Airport is located 3.5 miles east of Port Clinton, which puts it close to Sandusky. It is one of the larger area airports and an easy fly-in.

NORWALK-HURON COUNTY AIRPORT

(🖱 huroncountyairport.com) The Norwalk-Huron County Airport is another option for private plane enthusiasts to fly in for their visit to Sandusky's playground. It is located three miles east of Norwalk, about a 25-minute drive from Sandusky. Hangar or tie-down space is available.

OTHER TRANSPORT

Visitors to Sandusky can opt to travel the region in style and hire a limousine if they are so inclined.

TOM'S CRUZ

(🖰 **tomscruz.com**) Tom's Cruz Limousine Service in Sandusky markets a broad range of services with a range of sizes in limousines. Their services cover both group functions and individual needs, including airport runs from Cleveland Hopkins Airport and other local airports.

LOCAL SERVICES

When traveling, there are certain services and places people often need, ranging from the post office to medical facilities, or care for a pet or assisted living animal that is traveling along.

U.S. POST OFFICES

In addition to providing mailing services, the post office is often a source to find a location and assist with forwarded mail for those taking an extended vacation. The following are some of the area post offices: **Sandusky** *(2220 Caldwell St.* ☎ *419.626.5525)*; **Marblehead** *(606 Prairie St.* ☎ *418.798.4444)*; **Huron** *(378 Main St.* ☎ *419.433.5630)*; **Put-in-Bay** *(425 Langram Rd.* ☎ *419.285.4641)*; **Kelleys Island** *(427 W. Lakeshore Dr.* ☎ *419.746.2351)*.

POLICE DEPARTMENTS

For emergencies always dial 911. If needed, tourists can contact the police departments in **Sandusky** *(Police Gen. Business: 222 Meigs St.* ☎ *419.627.5863* 🖰 *ci.sandusky.oh.us/police/directory.htm)*; **Put-in-Bay** *(431 Catawba Ave.* ☎ *419.285.4121* 🖰 *put-in-baypolice.org)*; and **Marblehead** *(513 W. Main St.* ☎ *419.798.5881)*.

U.S. COAST GUARD STATION

(606 Prairie St., Lakeside, Marblehead ☎ 419.798.4444
🖱 wxusa.com/wx1/Marblehead+Coast+Guard+Station-OH.htm)
Boaters should be aware of how and where to reach the local
Coast Guard. Lake Erie is infamous as the most treacherous
of the Great Lakes. Storms arise quickly, as do wind changes
and rough waters. The Coast Guard is an important resource.
Check the Web site for weather reports and advisories.

MEDICAL SERVICES

Two area hospitals serving the Sandusky area are **Firelands
Regional Medical Center** *(1111 Hayes Ave., Sandusky*
☎ *419.626.7455* 🖱 *firelands.com)* and **Fisher-Titus Medical
Center** *(272 Benedict Ave., Norwalk* ☎ *800.489.3862/
419.668.8101* 🖱 *ftmc.com).*

PET CARE

There are several veterinary practices in the area and two full-
service practices known to be receptive to emergencies and
new patients. **Animal Clinic of Sandusky** *(405 E. Perkins
Ave., Sandusky* ☎ *419.625.2484)* is a full-service animal hospital
and companion care animal clinic. About 25 minutes east of
Sandusky is **Amherst Animal Hospital** *(1425 Cooper Foster
Park Rd., Amherst* ☎ *440.282.5220* 🖱 *amherst-animal-hospital.com).*
This full-service animal hospital is open daily except Sunday,
with kennel, boarding, and grooming services also provided.

ABOVE AND BEYOND SPA

(14006 Liberty Ave. Vermilion ☎ 440.967.7895) For personal
pampering services, a short drive east from Sandusky on the
Lake Road (Route 6) is the Above and Beyond Spa. This is

a full-service, unisex Aveda salon and spa, which offers the works, from hair and nails to facials and make-up, massage, sauna, and steam shower. Appointments are usually required but walk-ins can sometimes be accommodated. Calling ahead is the best way to be assured of good service. Packages are available and there is often a special promotion or open house going on. If you want to include a spa day as part of your vacation, set up a group event such as a wedding party, or if you simply want to have some fun with a "make-over," this establishment comes highly recommended for service, cleanliness, and up-to-date knowledge of trends and fashion.

SEASONS AND TEMPERATURES

Some places, especially on the Islands, close down completely in the winter season. Others remain open on a limited basis year-round or re-open for holidays and certain weekends. Nearly all are subject to change. Some are "officially" closed but may be amenable to a private booking on a limited basis. Therefore, it is best to make no assumptions and directly contact a place of interest and ask questions about specific arrangements, rates, and timing. Most of the small accommodations listed in this book are in business to accommodate customers; most will go out of their way to meet special requests if they can.

SPRING AND SUMMER

Summertime is by far the most popular time to visit Sandusky, when temperatures peak at about 82°F in July. **Cedar Point Amusement Park** - the top draw - is open from May through October. The waters of Lake Erie can reach the low 70s in the summer.

FALL AND WINTER

Wintertime can bring about some real bargains, but tourism is low and many of the major attractions are closed. Sandusky winters are extremely cold, with temperatures dropping to 20°F or lower. The water of Lake Erie is freezing in winter – just over 32°F. In general, to experience the best of Sandusky, plan on visiting during the warmer months.

The interest of a popular, local TV weather celebrity in a small fuzzy caterpillar was the genesis for the Woollybear Festival.

Festivals and Events

Something is always going on year-round in the Sandusky area and Islands. Dates for many of the events change annually. If you plan on attending any of the festivities to be held on the Islands, ferry, private boat, or air transport may be necessary.

BLESSING OF THE FLEET

(☻ put-in-bay.com) The Blessing of the Fleet is held at Put-in-Bay on South Bass Island, usually in late April. This special annual event signals the official beginning of the year's new fishing – and tourist – season. Ships, boats, ferries, water taxis, the U.S. Coast Guard, police water cruisers, and all other floating participants line up to receive prayers and holy water for the Annual Blessing of the Fleet. Helicopters and airplanes pass overhead to take part in the occasion. The annual celebration includes a parade, music, and frolic, as well as thanksgiving for another year on the water. Check the Web site for specific scheduling information.

FOURTH OF JULY AT PUT-IN-BAY

(☻ put-in-bay.com) Something fun is always cooking at Put-in-Bay, but July 4th holds a special tradition. This is a three-day weekend extravaganza of entertainers, fireworks, parties, and concerts. Details for each year's celebration are available on the Put-in-Bay Web site. Book well ahead to stay over on the island or for dockage, and expect lines and crowds for the ferries.

I-LYA SAILBOAT RACES AT PUT-IN-BAY

(🖱 put-in-bay.com) This four-day festival has been held every mid-to-late summer at South Bass Island for over 100 years. Outstanding colorful sailboats line up to begin racing on Monday of Race Week. Viewing of the race is from the west side of the island. There is a special events' schedule on the Web site with details to help you plan ahead if you want to attend.

OHIO BIKE WEEK

(🖱 ohiobikeweek.com) Calling all Harleys for a ten-day bike rally at bike-central Sandusky! Formerly the North Coast Thunder Rally, Ohio Bike Week has become an all-out, well-organized rally of racing events plus entertainment at various venues, ranging from downtown Sandusky to surrounding areas. The event is usually held in June.

KELLEYS ISLAND ANNUAL 10K AND 5K RUN

(☎ 419.746.2360 🖱 kelleysislandchamber.com) Kelleys Island five- and ten-K charity runs are a popular tradition and draw participants between 13 and over 70 years of age from far and wide. The races are usually held on a Sunday in June and also include a one-mile race, **Fun Day**. Contact Kelleys Island Chamber of Commerce for details and dates.

KELLEYS ISLAND FOLIAGE AND FEATHERS FESTIVAL

(Kelleys Island Audubon Club, PO Box 42, Kelleys Island 🖱 kelleysislandnature.com) Kelleys Island has been designated an Ohio Important Bird Area (IBA). The island includes a park preserve area. The Foliage and Feathers Festival offers bird and fall enthusiasts the opportunity to get out in late September to enjoy a full day of migrating song birds as they prepare to fly south. It is a pretty time to be on Kelleys Island. Follow the Web site for the dates of this annual event, which is held at **North Pond State Nature Preserve**.

ERIE COUNTY FAIR

(3110 Columbus Ave., Sandusky ⬤ eriecountyohiofair.com) Who doesn't love a fair in America's heartland? Well organized and operated by the Erie County Agricultural Society, the Erie County Fair offers traditional county fair activities and atmosphere. Held in August each year at the fairgrounds, the fair covers an ambitious schedule of traditional competitive events with a special focus on opportunities for the youth. There is always something enjoyable at the county fair. Check the Web site for specific dates and events for the year ahead.

MILAN MELON FESTIVAL

(⬤ milanmelonfestival.org) Milan, home of Thomas Edison, is located on Routes 113 and 250, just a short drive south of Sandusky on Route 250. Usually held in late August, the Milan Melon Festival celebrates the area's sweet harvest of watermelons and muskmelons with a host of activities, from the crowning of its young queen to its popular parade that winds through the town's sleepy, picturesque streets. Milan is an old small town and it has retained its traditional Americana look and feel. Parade day is a step back in time for all who attend. Races, contests (who's the most beautiful baby?), watermelon ice cream, and all sorts of other vendors fill the streets. The atmosphere is laidback and the people are friendly.

WOOLLYBEAR FESTIVAL

(⬤ vermilionohionews.homestead.com/ChamberofCommerce.html)

The interest of a popular, local TV weather celebrity in a small fuzzy caterpillar was the genesis for what has become a huge festival, and an ingrained annual fall tradition in Vermilion, which is a short shoreline drive east of Sandusky. This event draws people from virtually everywhere in numbers up to 100,000 in a single day.

Cleveland TV meteorologist, Dick Goddard, mentioned on air one year that the thickness of the rings of fur of the local orange and black "woolly bear" caterpillar found in the fall forewarned an especially cold winter. The wider the black ring, the colder would be the winter. From this prediction was born Dick Goddard's idea for the Woollybear Festival. A host of fun events, particularly enjoyable for children, are held on this occasion. The town literally closes down for the day's activities, such as woollybear races (how DO they get those caterpillars to head in the same direction and stay in their lanes?), kids' best woollybear costumes contest, and kids' races, all climaxed with the festival's keynote event – the huge Woollybear Parade. Participants from everywhere, it seems, come to join the parade. There is plenty of food, TV personalities, kids' events, live music concerts, and booths selling crafts, plus all the downtown stores are open for business too. Shuttle service assists parking and restroom facilities are provided. For more information and each year's date and schedule of specific events, check the Web site.

FESTIVAL OF THE FISH

The Festival of the Fish is another large event celebrated in Vermilion each year on Father's Day weekend. Highlights include a five-K run and a lighted boat parade on the Vermilion River at dusk. There is the Sunday street parade, sand castle contest, firefighters' water fight, lots of food, live music, and other activities to enjoy, including, of course, an abundance of fresh Lake Erie perch. **Main Street Marketplace** is set up during the Fish Festival weekend too, featuring a cornucopia of wares such as handmade wood items, jewelry, clothing, artwork, and other unique items that are fun to look at – and fun to buy.

SANDUSKY ANNUAL EVENTS SCHEDULE

(⏽ **cityofSandusky.com**) Sandusky Parks and Recreation and other city groups schedule special non-recurring events year-round. Information about these events is published on the Web site.

*When Sandusky was established sometime
in 1817, it was a wild, untamed place,
with main accessibility possible only via
lakes and waterways.*

Sandusky Area History

The name "Sandusky" means "at the cold water" in Wyandotte. When the first Europeans ventured into the Northwest Territory as explorers, trappers, and hunters, they found huge trees concealing a twilight world beneath their canopies, large marshes and prairie grasses, a land rich in wildlife, and the waters of the Great Lake with the rivers and streams dumping into it teeming in fish. It was a land inhabited, revered, and fought over by native tribes, notable among them the Eries, Iroquois, Wyandottes, Ottawas, and Hurons. Settlers arriving later would clear the great trees, turning soil that would provide bountiful harvests of grapes for wine making, grain, fruit, vegetables, and minerals for constructing roads and buildings.

Connecticut owned a large section of the Northwest Territory bordering Lake Erie. In 1786, Connecticut granted its land to the U.S. government as part of the Northwest Ordinance of 1787. However, Connecticut carved out for itself a portion of its land holdings in the Northwest Territory in what is now northern Ohio, calling it the Connecticut Western Reserve. Approximately 500,000 acres of the Western Reserve holds its own place in the history of the country's development. This area, the "Firelands," or "Sufferers' Lands," was saved for Connecticut's citizens who lost their homes and property to the fires set by the British troops who swept through and burned out whole towns during the American Revolution. The Ohio Corporation was formed to distribute property in the Firelands to eligible applicants from Connecticut. Settlement of the Firelands under this program began in earnest after the War of 1812. Sandusky, Ohio rests in the upper northwest corner of the Firelands.

During the early days of the settlement, the area that would become Sandusky was a British military and trading outpost. A decisive naval battle fought against the British in the War of 1812 took place on Lake Erie near Sandusky by South Bass Island in Put-in-Bay harbor under the command of Commodore Oliver Hazard Perry. It was in that victory that Perry wrote the famous words, "We have met the enemy and he is ours."

BEATTY AND COOKE – TWO EARLY SANDUSKY SCIONS

One of the people who came from Connecticut to Sandusky as part of the Firelands migration was an Irish immigrant named John Beatty who led a group of 14 people to the area in 1814. Sandusky was officially established circa 1817. In those days it was a wild place yet to be tamed, its main accessibility by the lake and waterways. Beatty was to become Mayor of Sandusky from 1833 to 1836. He was known for his temper and his unmitigated stand against slavery. A member of the Methodist church in Sandusky, he withdrew his membership in 1835 when the church voted against hosting an anti-slavery speaker. Beatty immediately proceeded to found his own Methodist church on Washington Square (all this during his term as Mayor). This was at a time long before anti-slavery sentiments had become common or politically popular in the country. After Beatty's death, his church disbanded. Its building served as a hospital during the 1849 cholera epidemic in the city. It was used again as a church after that until it was eventually demolished.

Eleutheros Cooke also came to Sandusky at the very beginning. His son, Jay, later described his father's arrival in the Sandusky area (as quoted by Oberholtzer in *Jay Cooke Financier of the Civil War* at 5), giving a flavor for Sandusky of the early 1800s:

> "[I]n due time [my father] reached Bloomingville, a spot about eight miles south of the present Sandusky. Here houses were erected and my brother Pitt was born in 1819. To the south of this village was a vast prairie, covered with waving grass, with herds of deer and wolves and innumerable flocks of wild turkeys, prairie chickens, etc. I have often listened to my father's stories of these things and particularly to the account of the journey in the winter from Madison and the many escapes from Indians, bears, and wolves. To the north of Bloomingville stretched an unbroken forest to Sandusky Bay and this was also the home of deer and other game. This whole region was the paradise of the Indians. Sandusky bay was at certain periods in the spring and fall covered with wild fowl and its waters were full of every variety of lake and river fish. The Indians here were Ottawas and Wyandottes and the district was known as the Firelands."

THE MAKING OF SANDUSKY

Organized development of Sandusky grew steadily. Unlike most towns of its era, the original plat was not laid out in the traditional parallel block fashion, but upon the pattern of the Masonic symbol of Square and Compass (said to be the only city so expressly designed). It was surveyed and designed by Hector Kilbourne, who also named many of the streets for prominent persons from the country's history at the time. Because of the unusual layout of the major design of the city, the streets run off at different angles and circle around in unexpected ways. For this reason, visitors today are advised to navigate the city with a well-marked street map or GPS in hand.

In 1838, Ohio made Sandusky the county seat of Erie County, which it remains today. By the mid-1800s, Sandusky was connected to the rest of the country by two railroads and its busy Great Lakes harbor. It was an important economic center for transport of coal, wheat, and other produce of the country's midwest. The city attracted entrepreneurs who established diverse manufacturing businesses. This was the period of great change and economic flourish in the city's history.

The city of Sandusky has served many roles in U.S. history: important stop on the Underground Railroad as a shore portal to Canada; transportation hub by ship, road, and rail; smugglers' attraction in the Prohibition era; commercial and competitive sport-fishing center; conservation area and tourist mecca.

The temptations for profit during Prohibition were great along Ohio's North Coast, where boats could slip out of harbors and hidden inlets and make the short run to Canada across the western end of Lake Erie. Occasionally the federal net caught big fish in its battle against profiteering. On July 29, 1925, the *Elyria Chronicle-Telegram* reported the arrest by federal warrants of Sandusky Probate Judge, John E. Tanney, along with 19 others as a result of undercover work by a federal agent in Sandusky, Vermilion, and Port Clinton, in an effort to "virtually stop the flow of whiskey and beer coming from Canada in high-powered yachts and speed boats."

Whether one is a history buff, an avid sports enthusiast, a serious fisherman, a boater, a bird-watcher, an amusement park thrill seeker, or a vacationer looking for an escape into quiet rest, relaxation, and sightseeing, visitors will likely find an outlet for their interests in the Sandusky area. The city boasts parks, museums, marinas, and, of course, the great **Cedar Point Amusement Park**. The area also offers many other natural attractions, shopping, island getaways, and scenic hideaways. There is something here for every kind of tourist.

By 1918, Cedar Point became well-known as "The Queen of American Watering Places."

Cedar Point

A peninsula jutting out into Lake Erie from Sandusky is today a famous and ultra-valuable piece of real estate known as Cedar Point. Always a natural site for fishing, the tip of the peninsula also became the location for a lighthouse station in 1838. During those early years, following land settlement of the Firelands, the large cedar trees that gave the peninsula its name were harvested for building. Some were lost in Lake Erie storms. Cedars no longer crowd the Point today. People do.

Please Note: Cedar Point attractions, for the most part, are seasonal. If you plan on visiting in the winter or off-season, contact the park in advance to see if the attraction(s) you want to experience will be available during your visit.

CEDAR POINT AMUSEMENT PARK ✪ Must See!

(One Cedar Point Dr., ☎ *419.627.2350* 🖋 *cedarpoint.com)* By far the most popular attraction on Cedar Point is the mammoth **Cedar Point Amusement Park**. Owned by Cedar Fair (which operates several parks across the United States), Cedar Point is the crown jewel of Sandusky-area tourism. At 364 acres, Cedar Point has more rides than any other amusement park in the world. Nicknamed "America's Roller Coast," the park has 75 rides, including 17 roller coasters, as well as shops, shows, and other attractions. It is primarily a summertime attraction, with an operating season between May and October, peaking in visitors from June-August.

Cedar Point is so iconic that it has been named "The Best Amusement Park in the World" for 12 years in a row by an *Amusement Today* poll. In fact, several rides at Cedar Point have attained a distinction as being the "best," or the "tallest," or the "fastest" in the world. Visitors primarily come in droves for the thrilling roller coasters, year after year. That's what Cedar Point is known for.

CEDAR POINT HISTORY

When a small railroad established an easier transport connection out onto the peninsula in 1867, the landscape of Cedar Point changed forever. The lighthouse was rebuilt the same year. Tourism was born on Cedar Point, which by 1918 would become well-known as "The Queen of American Watering Places."

Development started with the construction of bath houses to take advantage of the sandy beach and inviting picnic areas, for the peninsula provided a breezy haven from the inland and city summer heat. Subsequently, Cedar Point amusement activities expanded each year, drawing both day-trippers and vacationers who came to stay for weeks at a time in the cottages and hotels that sprang up on-site and in Sandusky city.

People poured into Cedar Point by rail, steamship, and eventually by car. Concerts and dances became regular summer events at Cedar Point in the late 19th and early 20th centuries. People would travel to Cedar Point on the *R. B. Hayes* steamer to enjoy the entertainment for the day and head back in the evening.

The *R.B. Hayes* was a steam-driven ferry that connected the Cedar Point peninsula to Sandusky's transport hub at the bottom of Columbus Avenue, where tourists embarked from the train depot and street cars. No doubt this access was the key to promoting the peninsula's tourism. From its first year in 1876, the *R.B. Hayes* faithfully served Cedar Point for years, several days a week.

At the end of the 19th century, Cedar Point's future began to wane as a watering hole for tourists and conventioneers. Then there was an infusion of cash and vision from George Arthur Boeckling when he arrived in Sandusky. With Boeckling's involvement, the Cedar Point Pleasure Resort & Company purchased the site for an alleged $256,000 – no small investment for that time. Soon the *R.B. Hayes* alone could not keep up with the crowds, and other steamboats were called into service over the years. Another steamship ferry was the *G.A. Boeckling*.

The ferries and excursion train were needed to transport the crowds of people who flocked to Cedar Point by rail and water from Detroit, Cleveland, Toledo, Columbus, Dayton, Cincinnati, and points beyond. Weekends were a big draw for Cedar Point tourism. Then came a flurry in 1901 when the laws banning Sunday liquor threatened to hurt Cedar Point's weekend business. Newspapers state-wide commented and commiserated on the park management's announcement that it would not open because of its expected loss of revenue under the Sunday liquor ban. Such an extreme interruption appears not to have happened, however, or in any case, the situation ultimately did not impede business on the Point for long.

Thereafter, newspaper notices and articles reported continuous happenings on at Cedar Point throughout the early 20th century. According to the *Sandusky Star Journal*, on June 20,

1921, the "largest crowd of the season" gathered at Cedar Point on Sunday. The article further reported:

"During the day hundreds of people went to the resort by automobile and boat. Many tourists from all 'parts of the country were registered at the Hotel Breakers over Saturday night and Sunday, The Cedara hotel also was filled with visitors over the weekend. The steamer Arrow carried an excursion party from Lorain of about 200 people. An excursion train of seven coaches came over the B. & O. from Akron, arriving here at 10:30 o'clock and leaving at 7 p. m. There were 119 passengers."

The article gives a flavor for Cedar Point's draw of crowds and its allure as a place for fun, thrills, and a touch of the exotic.

Cedar Point, midway during the early 20th century, became the hurley burley of carnival shows, games of skill, and cunning illusion. Fortune tellers, the bizarre, and the frightening populated the park's attractions. The genteel pace of the 19th-century bath house, cottage, and music era had evolved into the sideshow world. Still, Cedar Point's beach attracted the vacationers escaping the city heat, and the Great Pavilion had its dances, though the times were changing.

In the 1950s Cedar Point's land was divided between a state bird sanctuary, the **Sheldon Marsh Nature Preserve**, and a developer's vision of "Disneyland of the Midwest." In the decades that followed, the amusement park grew and morphed into the showpiece of today's Cedar Fair L.P. conglomerate, in constant competition with itself in successive years for ever bigger and greater heart-stopping rides to wow the thrill-seeking public.

ATTRACTIONS IN THE PARK

Cedar Point Amusement Park evolved from a carney show, beach, and big-band dance entertainment center in its Grand Pavilion, to a thrill-seeking extravaganza of increasingly creative rides and thrill shows. In 1978, Cedar Point debuted the **Gemini**, a record-setting roller coaster for height, steepness, and speed, followed by the **Magnum XL-200** in 1989, the **Mean Streak** in 1990, the **Raptor** in 1994 (an inverted roller coaster), and the gravity-defying straight-up **Mantis** in 1996.

In 2000, Cedar Point again opened with another record setter, the 300-foot high **Magnum Force**. Other high-thrill rides include the **Blue Streak** roller coaster, **Cedar Creek Mine Ride**, **Corkscrew**, **Disaster Transport**, **Iron Dragon**, **Jr. Gemini**, **Maverick**, **Top Thrill Dragster**, **Wicked Twister**, **Wildcat**, and **Woodstock Express**. All these rides command long lines of people waiting for their few seconds of thrilling body blasts that seemingly defy the rules of gravity and balance, creating a combination of raw fear and pure adrenaline rush, all rolled into ultimate delight for those with a strong stomach. The public puts its trust – and pocketbook – into the adrenaline-pumping risks offered by these rides at Cedar Point.

The "big rides" have height requirements that prohibit participation of small children for safety reasons. For the youngsters there are other rides smaller in scope. For those seeking more leisurely entertainment, there are more sedate theme adventures to experience in the park. The less death-defying pursuits include the beach, water activities, games, food, and sights – and more food – plus the endless stream of humanity for those who enjoy people-watching – and more food. Cedar Point has been known for over a century for its famous French fries and few children leave without devouring (and happily wearing) sticky mountains of cotton candy.

It is difficult *not* to find something to do or entertain in Cedar Point's entertainment venues, but the cost of the experience is not cheap. Just as the Magnum Force is not for the faint of heart, neither is the price of Cedar Point admission. There are season passes and reduced rates for evening entries. Discount tickets are available through package deals offered at the Cedar Point-owned accommodations. Special attractions usually are planned during the month of October through the first week of November for Halloween weekends ("HalloWeekends"). Check the prices for each new season. Also, there are usually special rates offered for senior citizens and those with military ID. Children under two can enter free of charge.

Use good sense and advance planning in choosing from the many options at the Cedar Point parks in order to get the most value of fun for the price. There are many types of entertainment to choose, ranging from the relaxing and low-key to the highest thrill level. Whatever one's pleasure though, be prepared for lots of walking and long lines, especially at peak times on summer days, holidays, and weekends.

The most consistent complaint of Cedar Point Park visitors is the standing in long lines for the rides. This means time in the park, for which one pays the high price of admission, is consumed in a lot of standing around waiting. For many people though, that ultimate thrill of the top rides is worth the wait. For others, the wait outweighs the cost and causes frustration. Some enterprising folks have been known to pay people to wait in line for them. This practice carries a risk. The perception of someone "taking cuts" ahead is never well received by those trapped in a long line on a hot day.

The key to enjoying Cedar Point's many attractions is doing one's homework in advance and planning to take maximum advantage of available discounts. Timing park visits so as to minimize the likelihood of the longest lines for waiting can reduce frustration at the park. Another consideration is parking, which is a separate cost added onto the price of admission, unless one is staying in Cedar Point accommodations that include parking as an amenity. Not all the Cedar Point accommodations venues may include park parking, but they may provide shuttle service. Do not take either for granted. Check specifically for the availability of these courtesies.

Health tips: Wear and replenish sunscreen and beware of dangers of dehydration and fatigue during a day at the park, especially for children.

OTHER CEDAR POINT ATTRACTIONS

The main amusement park is not the only attraction at Cedar Point. A water park, mini-golf, and other attractions are nearby and easily accessible from the main park.

SOAK CITY ✪ Must See!
(🔍 soakcity.cedarpoint.com) Soak City is an 18-acre water park located next to the main **Cedar Point Amusement Park**. It offers 15 water participation elements, each with its own height restrictions and rules. There are lifeguards, food

courts, and places to just stretch out and work on one's tan, read a book, or people-watch. One of the greatest advantages of Soak City is its offering of something for everyone. It is not "just" a water park.

Soak City includes an array of water walks, floats, slides, waves, and pools. Many of the attractions require children to be accompanied by an adult and wear life vests if they are shorter than the minimum height requirements (ranging from 46 to 52 inches). There is the **Choo Choo Lagoon** though, strictly for children, and the **Bubbles Swim-up Bar Pool**, strictly for those who are 21 or over.

Soak City also offers 24 private 10 x 10 foot cabanas by advance reservation on a "first come first served" basis. These are located near the **Breakers Wave Pool** and include a private table for food and drink service and chaise lounge seating for four.

Like Cedar Point, there are discount opportunities, evening and special admission rates, and additional cabana rates for Soak City. Closing times also vary, so it is wise to check ahead not only for rates, but also for open hours on the days one might plan to visit.

CHALLENGE PARK ✪ Must See!

(⚫ cedarpoint.com) Located between **Cedar Point Amusement Park** and **Soak City**, Challenge Park is its own self-contained entertainment center consisting of two 18-hole mini-golf courses, two go-cart raceways, the **Skycoaster** and the **Skyscraper**. Cedar Point admission is not required to get into Challenge Park, but each of Challenge Park's activities has its own cost.

The miniature golf courses are set up with water and land hurdles that one must overcome to successfully navigate their 18-hole challenges. The go-cart tracks are programmed for medium and adult driver levels of challenge racing.

The Skycoaster is called the **Ripcord**, which, as it sounds, is akin to a bungee jump thrill experience. Daredevils are hoisted some 15 stories in the air to "fly" straight down 150 feet at around 80 miles per hour.

New in 2008, the Skyscraper ride is yet another in Cedar Point's long line of thriller coups in the amusement park industry. It is a two-armed ride, like a giant propeller, that spins its victims in a full circle clockwise and counterclockwise, carrying four riders at a time (two on each arm). These propeller arms spin 16 stories into the air up to 55 mph over a time span of about two minutes. Include this one in the category of rides not for the faint of heart or weak of stomach. For additional fun, those who stay on the ground may watch the two-minute Skyscraper ride unfold in streaming video.

NORTH COAST PARASAIL & JET SKI

(☎ **419.627.2279** 🖳 **cedarpoint.com**) North Coast Parasail & Water Sports and Jet Ski offers rentals for parasailing and jet skiing on Lake Erie from Memorial Day to Labor Day, weather permitting. It is located outside the park behind the **Hotel Breakers**. Given the nature of Lake Erie's moods, planning for water sports is of necessity a day-to-day business. Check online or call for hours and new season prices. Park admission is not required. There is a parking fee for visitors who are not staying at the Breakers.

CEDAR POINT LODGING

For those vacationers who make the journey to the area with the express purpose of diving straight into the **Cedar Point Amusement Park**, there are several ideally situated lodging options, perfectly located to fulfill that objective with minimum travel time.

HOTEL BREAKERS

(1 Cedar Point Dr., Cedar Point, Sandusky ☎ 419.627.2106 🌐 cedarpoint.com) Hotel Breakers is a historic fixture at Cedar Point, snuggled against Lake Erie's beach with its own convenient entrances in walking distance from **Cedar Point Amusement Park**, **Soak City**, and **Challenge Park**. Hotel guests are offered a one-hour early entry into Cedar Point and the popular rides such as Millennium Force, Raptor, Skyhawk, Iron Dragon, and Planet Snoopy before general admission opens to the public. Guests will still encounter lines for these rides, but comparatively less than when the rest of the public swarms in. Though no five-star hotel, Hotel Breakers is updated and family friendly (such as its "Peanuts" suites), and offers many of the conveniences people would expect of a resort atmosphere. The rooms may not be high-end luxury, but some deluxe options are available in the newer "Tower," where the rooms are comfortable and well serviced, as are the rooms in the older sections of the hotel.

For most visitors, the main attraction of Hotel Breakers is location. Set out on the lake and in the middle of the action, the hotel still manages to be an oasis of peace and quiet and a place to escape the madding crowd and cacophony of the huge amusement park. This is especially convenient for families.

Also, guests at the hotel will not lose the car in a parking lot the size of an ocean. Hotel Breakers also provides complimentary shuttle service. In addition to the hotel's beach access, there are two outdoor pools, one indoor pool, and three whirlpool spas. A poolside deli and coffee shop are on-site and other restaurants are readily accessible nearby. Complimentary WiFi is available in the lobby, rotunda, and conference area.

In addition to its convenience, Hotel Breakers offers the cachet of historical ambience for those who like the feeling of being a part of history, given that the hotel dates back to the early days of Cedar Point.

Hotel Breakers offers several vacation packages and weekend getaway options with discount tickets to the parks, extra entertainment, and additional amenities included. Most of the hotel packages include "munch money" to spend for food on-site. Room rates vary according to the season and by type of room. Advance reservations are highly recommended. Viewing of rooms and making reservations can be done online.

For those seeking ultra-modern and new accommodations, one of the newer Cedar Point accommodations might be considered, such as **Castaway Bay**, which is off site, but still quite close to the park.

BREAKERS EXPRESS HOTEL

(1 Cedar Point Dr., Cedar Point, Sandusky ☎ 419.627.2106 ☖ cedarpoint.com) Another Cedar Point-owned hotel is the Breakers Express Hotel, located on the Cedar Point Causeway, not far from Cedar Point. A more typical "express hotel" building, this option offers an outdoor pool and whirlpool spa. It also offers complimentary WiFi in the lobby and game room, but not in the guest rooms. As the name implies, this is a scaled-down version of the full-service amenities offered at **Hotel Breakers**. However, its room rates will generally include discounted tickets to Cedar Point (which is a short drive away). Higher package rates may be available to include tickets and breakfast at **Castaway Bay** a block down the road. Rates tend to be lower than **Hotel Breakers**, but are by no means cheap; many consider them to be overpriced. Cedar Point parking fees are not included and there is no shuttle service to the parks. Most rooms are double queen, with rollaway beds available at an extra charge to accommodate an extra person in a room. Advance reservations are recommended.

LIGHTHOUSE POINT

(1 Cedar Point Dr., Cedar Point, Sandusky ☎ 419.627.2106 ● cedarpoint.com) Lighthouse Point, another Cedar Point-owned lodging option, offers something different and quaint for Cedar Point-bound enthusiasts. This is an option for someone who likes the idea of camping, but not the idea of totally roughing it. Lighthouse Point is a community of 64 cottages and 60 cabins settled around the historic **Cedar Point Lighthouse**. The accommodations, however, are 21st century. Each one-story efficiency-style cottage is air conditioned, customized to comfortably accommodate up to six people, and has two TVs, a full bathroom, microwave, small refrigerator, coffee maker, and grill on the outside front deck.

Inland from the cottage group, the one-story cabins are arranged around a small pond. These also can sleep up to six people, plus two more in a small loft area (loft bedding not supplied). The cabins offer the same living amenities as the cottages, except instead of an outside porch, there is a private patio outside with picnic table and grill.

A one-hour early entry to Cedar Point, discount tickets, and package deals are available with the Lighthouse Point bookings. Advance reservations are recommended.

Utilizing the maximum capacity sleeping arrangements offered by these cabins and cottages means sharing tight quarters, but also gives the advantage of sharing the nightly pricey rate. The premise for the Lighthouse community is a place to sleep and hang out on a break from the full-time occupation of playing out in the amusement parks and enjoying other activities of the area.

CAMPER VILLAGE

(1 Cedar Point Dr., Cedar Point, Sandusky ☎ 419.62.2106 ⬤ cedarpoint.com) Set up like a wheel, with the laundry, bath, and other group facilities as the hub, Camper Village is an RV site for visitors who want to drive their own lodging within walking distance to **Cedar Point**, **Soak City**, and **Challenge Park**. Located adjacent to **Lighthouse Point**, it currently provides 283 total RV sites; 59 of these have full hook-ups. TV hook-ups are available and pets are allowed. Camper Village is open from May through October. Cedar Point Park discount packages are available along with the early park admission entry options offered at other Cedar Point hotels.

CASTAWAY BAY RESORT HOTEL AND SPA ✪ Must See!

(1 Cedar Point Dr., Cedar Point, Sandusky ☎ 419.627.2106 ⬤ cedarpoint.com) Cedar Point's Castaway Bay Resort Hotel and Spa spins a Caribbean flavor into its ambience. This hotel offers both standard rooms and larger suites, plus a 38,000 square foot indoor water park (open year-round), arcade, shops, restaurants, a child-activity center, and its own marina. Large suites include one king, two doubles, and one queen sofa bed. Off season, Castaway Bay's water park availability may vary; inquire ahead when booking to be sure the water park will be open.

Like the other Cedar Point hotels, Castaway Bay offers an abundance of package options and in season, it offers early entry to the **Cedar Point Parks** for the Millennium Force, Raptor, Skyhawk, Iron Dragon, and Planet Snoopy rides. Most rooms have their own balconies or decks. Castaway Bay is close to Cedar Point, but is not within walking distance.

SANDCASTLE SUITES

(1 Cedar Point Dr., Cedar Point, Sandusky ☎ 419.627.2106 🖱 cedarpoint.com) Located out on the tip of the Cedar Point peninsula, the all-suite Sandcastle is in walking distance to **Cedar Point**, **Soak City**, and **Challenge Park**. This is its main allure, particularly given that it is not a luxurious hotel considering its price. The suites are not big or especially deluxe. Like the other Cedar Point lodging options, the expectation is that people are coming here to spend time at the parks, not in the hotel room. The rooms offer the basics, but will be crowded if they are filled to recommended maximum capacity. Three suites have in-suite hot tubs and connected decks or patios.

The views at Sandcastle are lovely, but if you are coming to Sandusky for a quiet getaway for rest and relaxation with a view, there are many other choices to stay at a better price with quainter ambience, and still include a day at Cedar Point in your itinerary.

Still, like the other Cedar Point-owned accommodations, the Sandcastle's location is attractive and convenient for serious theme park enthusiasts. Amenities offered to Sandcastle guests include water park passes, one-hour early entry into **Cedar Point Amusement Park**, outdoor pool and whirlpool spa, beach access, and tennis courts. Courtesy shuttle service is also available for amusement park access. For dining choices, the **Breakwater Café** and **Sand Bar** are on-site.

Outdoor Water Park at Kalahari

Indoor Wave Pool in Kalahari

Merry-Go-Round Museum

The Boy with the Boot

Old Woman Creek

Gull over Lake Erie

Lake Erie, near Marblehead

Put-in-Bay

Marblehead Lighthouse

LCA 08

Sandusky Bay

Wooden Coaster at Cedar Point

Steel Coaster at Cedar Point

Historic Ships in Lake Erie

Midway Carousel

Cedar Point Park Scene

Lake Erie is the most treacherous of the Great Lakes, with its unpredictable storms and rocky shores having been the bane of several ships and boats.

Other Area Attractions

Although Sandusky's North Coast Playground is perhaps most famous for Cedar Point, there are many other attractions and activities in the area to keep visitors busy. Fishing and boating are obvious draws for the Sandusky area. There are also other entertainment options for families as well as nature attractions.

WATER PARKS

As a summertime vacation destination, Sandusky has more than its share of water activities. A few large water park hotels are in the area, as well as some smaller places that are jumping onto the water park bandwagon.

FORT MACKENZIE, GREAT WOLF LODGE ✪ Must See!
(4600 Milan Rd., Route 250, Sandusky ☎ 866.679.9731
⬛ greatwolf.com) Great Wolf Lodge has become a popular getaway for families who come to enjoy its year-round indoor water park and large guest rooms. It is a self-enclosed themed water park, one of a chain of the Great Wolf Resorts located throughout the United States and Canada. Its water park, however, is open only to registered hotel guests. Located on Route 250 in Sandusky, Great Wolf is easily accessible from Route 2.

One of the more spectacular of the Great Wolf attractions is Fort Mackenzie. This contraption is four stories tall, styled as a "treehouse" fort the whole family can climb (and as such is able to include the younger children) to the water slides at the top. But the real kicker of this huge puzzle of bridges and slides, and nets and water sprays, is the periodic clang of a bell signaling that the 1,000 gallon reservoir at the top is about to dump its contents upon all in its path below.

Aside from the fort, Great Wolf does provide something for all ages. There is an arcade, a "lazy" river (as part of the indoor water park) for the less actively inclined, a temporary tattoo center, story time and clock tower show for young children, and an adults-only whirlpool, to name a few of the variety of offerings on hand to appeal to various age groups. Also see the "Accommodations" chapter for details about the Great Wolf Lodge.

KALAHARI WATERPARK RESORT AND KAHUNAVILLE

(7000 Kalahari Dr., Sandusky ⏻ kalahariresorts.com) Located south of Sandusky, off of Route 250, Kalahari is another themed indoor water park. There are some minor complaints that the Kahunaville restaurant food price is high for the quality and that some of the water activities are not always open due to short staffing. Despite the complaints, many patrons keep returning for second and third visits. Cleanliness of the rooms consistently gets high marks. The "wave" is one of the more popular water activities. Also see the chapter on "Accommodations" for details about the rooms and other hotel facilities available.

If a person wants to skip the Kalahari water activities and opt instead to partake in the restaurant, Kahunaville is kid friendly and making a reputation for huge desserts. This is a venue that is designed to entertain families. It is easily accessible from both Ohio Route 2 and the Ohio Turnpike.

RAIN QUALITY INN WATERPARK & SUITES

(1935 Cleveland Rd., Sandusky ☎ 419.626.6761/800.654.3364)
The Rain Quality Inn offers a smaller water park than the behe-
moths of **Great Wolf** and **Kalahari**, plus laser tag, an arcade,
and bowling alley as alternative and more affordable family
attractions. In addition, there is off-track horse race gambling for
the adults and food on the premises. The "Accommodations"
chapter has details about the rooms and suites.

MONSOON LAGOON WATER PARK

(1530 S. Danbury Rd., Port Clinton
🖱 **monsoonlagoonwaterpark.com)** Water parks are among the
most popular family-fun themes and the season, outdoor
Monsoon Lagoon adds its own twist to the craze. The goal
here is that no one stays dry. There are six waterslides, one
being the **Typhoon Rush Slide Tower**, which is three stories
of rushing water. The **Tree House** offers multi-level play
stations and **Pirates Cove** has its bumper boats. For little ones
too small for the big stuff, there is the **Little Squirts** pool. An
adult-only pool includes the obligatory Tiki bar. There is more
to do than just get soaked though. To add variety to its water
park activities, Monsoon Lagoon has its go-cart **Montego Bay
Raceway** and an 18-hole miniature golf course.

HISTORIC SITES AND MUSEUMS

Sandusky has always been proud of its history and heritage. There
are many places in and around the Sandusky and Ohio's North
Coast for an avid historian or curious onlooker to explore.

DIVE LAKE ERIE SHIPWRECKS ✪ Must See!

(🖰 ohioshipwrecks.org) Hundreds of shipwrecks lie at the bottom of Lake Erie, many of which have been identified for diving exploration. There is a concentration of such sites in the Sandusky area. Three submerged wrecks lie offshore near Kelleys Island – the *F.H. Prince, Adventure,* and *W.R. Hanna.* The *Isabella J. Boyce* lies off Middle Bass Island.

The *F.H. Prince* was a propeller steamer carrying sand and gravel. She lies approximately half a mile offshore of Kelleys Island, east of the island's airstrip. She caught fire and was run aground in 1911 by her captain H.H. Parsons, when an attempt to put out the fire failed. This site is popular for both scuba divers and snorklers and also serves well for smallmouth bass fishers.

The *Adventure* left port in Sandusky on October 6, 1903, bound for Kelleys Island. The boat caught fire at the Kelleys Island dock. Everyone aboard escaped, but all possessions were lost. The steam tug *L.P. Smith* towed the burning *Adventure* out into the island's North Bay, a maneuver which saved the dock and a schooner in port from catching fire. Imagining the terrifying scene this must have been underscores its heroic nature. The *Adventure* burned to the water line and sank, lying now as a wreck for divers' interest.

The *W.R. Hanna,* a scow-sailing schooner built in 1857 in Sandusky was wrecked ashore by a gale in 1886.

The *Isabella J. Boyce,* built in 1889, was a bulk freighter converted to a sandsucker, a ship used to harvest sand from the lake bottom. She foundered on the East Point Reef off Middle Bass Island and caught fire there in 1917.

Such locations abound in the area. The **Shipwrecks and Maritimes Tales** (🌐 *ohioshipwrecks.org*) Web site points enthusiasts to locations all over Lake Erie.

MARBLEHEAD LIGHTHOUSE ✪ Must See!
(Marblehead Lighthouse State Park, 110 Lighthouse Dr., Marblehead: Information contact: East Harbor State Park, 1169 North Buck Rd., Lakeside-Marblehead ☎ 419.734.4424)
It is no secret that Lake Erie is one of the most treacherous of the Great Lakes. Its unpredictable, sudden storms and rocky shores have claimed many ill-fated boats and ships. The Marblehead Lighthouse has protected ships and sailors from such a fate since 1822. As an historical landmark in Marblehead, which is close to Sandusky, the lighthouse also offers an attractive, scenic backdrop for both picnic and photo opportunities.

As the gull flies, Marblehead Lighthouse is approximately opposite Sandusky, just around Sandusky Bay, facing the lake. Once maintained and operated by an on-site keeper, the Marblehead light is now automatic, operated by the U.S. Coast Guard. Flashing every six seconds, its green light is visible for 11 nautical miles. The lighthouse and its keeper's house are surrounded by well-placed picnic tables anchored on huge, flat rocks, whose neighbors also provide seating opportunities for viewing the water and its island horizons with the great structure towering above. This place is a timeless, irresistible draw for artists, lovers, families, photographers, history buffs, vacationers, bird-watchers, and those who simply seek its quiet solitude for a few hours' escape.

A museum is located in the former keeper's house next to the lighthouse. Tours are usually conducted on weekday afternoons between May and August, and also from the second Saturday of June through October. It is recommended that visitors check ahead to confirm tour times.

Aside from the historical interest, the best offerings of this site are the picnicking opportunity and its restful, secluded ambience next to the water. Ample parking and restrooms are available on-site.

JOHNSON'S ISLAND

(🖱 johnsonsisland.org) Those with an interest in Civil War history can step back in time on Johnson's Island, a short distance west of Sandusky.

In 1861, the U.S. Army established a Civil War Prisoner of War Camp offshore on Johnson's Island to hold captured Confederate soldiers. The prison there was active from April 1862 to September 1865. The prison camp generated a primary source history of correspondence, diaries, records, photos, and other material memorialized in the **Johnson's Island Museum** now located on the mainland in Marblehead.

The citizens of Sandusky were by no means aloof from the P.O.W.s of Johnson's Island. On record at the U.S. Library of Congress is a letter petition from several prominent Sanduskians to President Abraham Lincoln on behalf of Mrs. Charles Frazier, seeking the parole of her husband from Johnson's Island.

Today, Johnson's Island is connected to the mainland by a causeway, and is exclusively occupied by private homes, with the notable exception of the Confederate Cemetery of 206 soldiers, who died in prison. The causeway access currently costs $1, so be sure to have $2 in hand (in dollars or quarters) to cross over to the island to visit the cemetery. The cemetery is the only place open to the public on Johnson's Island. Being private property, the island is not recommended for a family outing such as a picnic or beach walk. The drive over is of interest mainly for those who wish to see the cemetery as part of historical odyssey.

JOHNSON'S ISLAND MUSEUM

(414 West Main St., Marblehead 🖰 johnsonsisland.org) The museum is located on the mainland side. Johnson's Island Museum is where one can peruse the photographs and other memorabilia about the Johnson's Island Confederate prison history. The museum stays open during most afternoons on weekends and holidays from Memorial Day to Labor Day. There is no admission charge. Sometimes it is possible to make special arrangements for off-time visits.

MERRY-GO-ROUND MUSEUM ✪ Must See!

(301 Jackson St., Sandusky ☎ 419.626.6111 🖰 merrygoroundmuseum.org) The Merry-Go-Round Museum is a favorite with Sandusky visitors and residents alike. The museum is easily accessible in downtown Sandusky. The main attraction, without question, is the fully restored and operating antique *Allen Herschell Carrousel*, the museum's centerpiece, ready to carry visitors on a ride into the past delight of a bygone era. The carousel was originally manufactured at the Herschell Carrousel Factory in Tonawanda, New York (the site of another renowned carousel museum).

The Herschell Carrousel came to Sandusky without its original carved animals. The workings of the carousel were restored and the animals for it have been patiently carved in the traditional way with the original tools, funded by donations. Collectors have also placed valuable pieces on loan with the museum. The result is a functioning, authentic early 1900s carousel. Additional carousel items are on display throughout the museum. As an additional interest, visitors may watch carousel artisans at work demonstrating their skills during museum hours. Check the Web site or call for admission days, cost, and times.

MARITIME MUSEUM OF SANDUSKY

(125 Meigs St., Sandusky ☎ 419.624.0274

📱 sanduskymaritime.org) Located in downtown Sandusky, across from **Battery Park**, the Maritime Museum of Sandusky documents the history of Sandusky Bay, Lake Erie's shipping and fishing lore, and related subjects, including the early boats that serviced Cedar Point, such as the *G.A. Boeckling*. Check the Web site or call for information about admission charges and visiting hours, which vary seasonally.

FOLLETT HOUSE MUSEUM ✪ Must See!

(404 Wayne St., Sandusky ☎ 419.627.9608

📱 sandusky.lib.oh.us/follett_house) Now an adjunct to the **Sandusky Public Library**, the Follett House Museum was built as the Greek Revival-style, four-story home of Oran Follett. Follett was a prominent Sanduskian in his time, well placed in the management of the local bank and the Mad River Railroad. Later in life, he became obsessed with proving that Lord Bacon, not Shakespeare, wrote Shakespeare's plays.

Listed on the National Register of Historic Landmarks, Follett House is one of the many grand old houses that once lined the streets angling off Sandusky's downtown center at the turn of the 20th century. Within its preserved walls, the museum's purpose is to allow visitors and researchers a window into Sandusky's history through its industries, local society, daily life, and its role within the context of the events of each unfolding era of history.

At the top of the building, a widow's walk provides a panoramic view of the town and Sandusky Bay. For those who may want to follow up with even more specific research, including genealogical study, the library's **Archives Research Center** is at the main library a block away. Both Follett House and the Archives have been used by national scholars. Check the Web site or call to confirm open hours.

EDISON BIRTHPLACE MUSEUM ✪ Must See!

(9 Edison Dr., Milan ☎ 419.499.2135 ▯ tomedison.org) The small town of Milan, about a 15-minute drive down Route 250 from Sandusky, was the home of Thomas Edison – and is proud of it. Like the picturesque town itself, the small red-brick Edison House with its white picket fence appears from the outside as if it could not hold very much, but in fact generally surprises visitors with its "bigness" inside. The tour of Edison's birthplace and home is rich in historic detail and of interest to adults and children alike.

Though born there, Thomas Edison did not live long in Milan. His family moved to Port Huron, where his father was a lighthouse keeper. He was home-schooled by his mother and flourished under her attention. Though Edison's adult home was primarily in Menlo Park, New Jersey, he bought his birthplace in Milan in 1906 when the house had no electricity, a lapse which has since been remedied.

MILAN HISTORICAL MUSEUM ✪ Must See!

(10 Edison Dr., Milan ☎ 419.499.4968 🖥 milanhistory.org) Next door to Edison's Birthplace stands the Milan Historical Museum. Include lunch plans with a visit here, either with a self-packed picnic or at one of Milan's quaint restaurants. The Museum has an extensive series of exhibits and outdoor gardens and hosts many kid-friendly events throughout the year.

HISTORIC CHOLERA CEMETERY

(Harrison St., Sandusky) The Historic Cholera Cemetery is of interest to people who seek out historical sites and stories. One of Sandusky's defining qualities is its reverence for its history and appreciation for those who played a positive role in it. In 1849, a cholera outbreak decimated the population of Ohio. At that time, Sandusky's population was about 5,667. At the approach of the cholera outbreak, 3,500 are said to have fled the city. Of the remaining population, 400 succumbed to the disease. Because of the overwhelming number of simultaneous deaths and concerns about contagion, most of the dead had to be interred in a mass grave in a local cemetery, today commemorated as the Cholera Cemetery on Harrison Street in Sandusky.

During the epidemic's height, physicians came to Sandusky from all over Ohio and as far away as Pennsylvania to care for the sick. This was no small act of kindness. The travel alone was not easy in those times – to make the trip into a climate of plague was heroic beyond measure. A monument in their remembrance stands in the center of the cemetery. The Ohio Historical Society has also placed a plaque here, listing the physicians and people who selflessly served the sick when the epidemic hit. This plaque supplements the symbolic assurance of the monument that the courage of those people will not be forgotten and that the appreciation of the citizens of Sandusky will never diminish.

There are other old headstones at the cemetery unrelated to the cholera epidemic. Also buried here is William H. Hunter, a lawyer and local politician who was elected to the U.S. House of Representatives from 1837–39. According to the public record, and confirmed in the Library of Congress, Mr. Hunter died near Sandusky in 1842 of "mysterious circumstances."

ELEUTHEROS COOKE HOUSE MUSEUM AND GARDEN
⭐ Must See!

(1415 Columbus Ave., Sandusky ☎ 419.627.0640) Eleutheros Cooke, born in New York in 1787, came to Erie County in 1817. He was Sandusky's first lawyer and a U.S. Congressman. Cooke also invested heavily in real estate and railroads in the city. This house was his, built in 1843–44 at the corner of Columbus Avenue and Washington Row, where he lived until his death in 1864. In 1874 (some sources say 1879), the house was taken down and moved to 1415 Columbus Avenue, where it continued as a private residence until the 1950s. Like the **Follett House**, the Cooke House is considered an example of Greek Revival architecture. Now owned by the Ohio Historical Society, it has been kept as it was as a private home in the

1950s, and is filled with antiques. It is set within beautifully kept grounds, which feature a greenhouse.

Cooke's august legacy was carried forward by his son, Jay Cooke, who became a wealthy railroad magnate. Jay substantially financed the U.S. government during the Civil War. Through his efforts and financial genius, the U.S. came out of the war inevitably in debt but financially stable. Cooke also profited himself but his work in the war gave him the nickname, "financier of the Civil War."

SANDUSKY ON THE UNDERGROUND RAILROAD

(Lake Erie Shores and Islands Welcome Center, 4424 Milan Rd., State Route 250, Suite A, Sandusky ☎ 419.625.2984/ 800.255.3743) Prior to the Civil War, many people along the Sandusky area of Lake Erie were active in the Underground Railroad. Sandusky played a key role in this clandestine system of human connections, moving people against the law at great risk. As one of the Great Lakes ports close to the Canadian border and situated among several river systems, Sandusky, ideally located to receive refugees, was a major depot on the freedom trail. In her book *Uncle Tom's Cabin,* Harriet Beecher Stowe immortalized Sandusky as Eliza's family escape route.

Leading Sandusky officials, lawyers, socialites, businessmen, and lake captains, as well as quiet low-profile people, were all involved in the anti-slavery effort. One such advocate was George J. Reynolds, whose business was located at the northeast corner of Jackson and Madison Streets in downtown Sandusky, and believed to have been an Underground Railroad safe house. The officers of the ships *Arrow, United States, Mayflower,* and *Bay City*, which ran from Sandusky to Detroit, were known to be willing to help escaped slaves reach Canada. The Second Baptist Church at 315 Decatur Street was called "The First Anti-Slavery Baptist Church of Sandusky." Runaway slaves were brought into the city by armed men posing as hunters driving covered wagons concealing their "kill," a hunting party's common transport method.

Oran Follett (of the **Oran Follett House**) was an anti-slavery sympathizer, but concerned about the aspect of breaking the law. His wife, Eliza Follett, however, a tireless helper of the poor and afflicted, was more militant. She helped feed and clothe many escaped slaves on their way through Sandusky to Canada. It is reported that Eliza's response, when Oran expressed his concern to her about breaking the law forbidding aiding and abetting runaway slaves, was, "Husband, there is a higher law."

The first runaway slave known to receive sanctuary in Sandusky was a man who was owned by a gentleman named Riley. The slave arrived in Sandusky on foot in 1820, Riley in close pursuit. Captain P. Shephard hid the slave in C.W. Marsh's tavern for three days, literally under Riley's nose while he searched to no avail. The story goes that on the fourth day, a frustrated Riley took the steamer to Detroit, widening his search. Meanwhile Captain Shephard seized the opportunity to hide Riley's slave on his sailboat and head for Canada, where the man was safely freed. When Riley returned from Detroit, his slave was long gone.

Many of the actual Underground Railroad safe houses are now lost to the mists of time, but history unquestionably records Sandusky's commitment as a major "depot" on the Underground Railroad. The **Lake Erie Shores and Islands**

Welcome Center offers a brochure for a self-guided driving tour of the area for remaining sites that played a role in the Underground Railroad system. Although most of the actual sites active in those times no longer exist and those remaining are not readily open to the public, this driving tour still raises a heightened awareness of historical interest and assist visitors in becoming acquainted with the area. Visitors may also inquire about specific site information and the possibility of guided tours. There is no charge for the brochure, and a modest charge for a guided tour.

RUTHERFORD B. HAYES PRESIDENTIAL CENTER
⭐ Must See!

(Spiegel Grove in Fremont 🖱 rbhayes.org/visitors) The Rutherford B. Hayes Presidential Center stands as a beautiful preservation of the Hayes home at Spiegel Grove. Ohioan Rutherford B. Hayes was the 19th President of the United States (1877–1881). The Hayes family established his Presidential library as the first in the United States, inaugurating a historical tradition of preserving important presidential documents and personal memorabilia of a U.S. president. The Hayes library was opened in 1916 and has been expanded to shelve 70,000 volumes of books related to his times (known as the Gilded Age), his personal interests, genealogy, and place. The library has become a research center, not only of President Hayes' particular interests, but of the local area as well. It includes collections covering the history of northwest Ohio, the Lake Erie Islands, local history, and local government.

President Hayes' home, a 31-room mansion, and the **Dillon House**, a large period home in Fremont, have been kept in beautiful restoration as a museum treasure and event center. Members of the center may reserve rooms in the Dillon House for overnight stays. Visit the Web site for information about the center, its daily tours of the **Hayes Home** and **Hayes Museum**, and special events open to the public.

SPORTS AND RECREATION

From a thrilling speedway to a laidback city park, there are numerous options for Sandusky visitors to enjoy.

SANDUSKY SPEEDWAY MOTOR SPORTS PARK

(614 W. Perkins Ave., Sandusky ☎ Track: 419.625.4084; Cell: 440.213.7003 ✆ sanduskyspeedway.com) Stock-car racing enthusiasts may find their niche at Sandusky Speedway. The season runs April through October. There is a general admission price with special rates for a Pit Pass, plus special events pricing. It is best to check into the track's event schedule for admission rates, specific dates, and lap times. Sandusky Speedway also hosts go-carting events, generally in the fall. The Web site posts the track's event schedule.

GOODTIME I LAKE ERIE ISLAND CRUISES ✪ Must See!

(Goodtime Lake Erie Island Cruises, LLC, Jackson Street Pier, P.O. Box 60, Sandusky ☎ 800.446.3140/419.625.9692 ✆ goodtimeboat.com) The *Goodtime I* is a 355-passenger ocean-going cruiser that offers daily island-hopping lake tours with stops at Kelleys Island and Put-in-Bay (South Bass Island). During the season from Memorial Day through Labor Day, the *Goodtime I*'s Friday night schedule includes a party cruise to Kelleys Island complete with DJ. Headlined for "party animals," this cruise is limited to party-goers who are 21 years old. Also popular are the less restricted, more family-oriented Sunset cruises on Sandusky Bay on Tuesday evenings in July and August.

The *Goodtime I* departs from downtown Sandusky's Jackson Street Pier. Follow Columbus Avenue to the end, turn left on Water Street, right on Jackson Street, and then take a right on Shoreline Drive. Free parking is available at the Jackson Street Pier. Boarding begins in the mid-morning for the day cruises. Fares vary according to season; check the *Goodtime* Web site for fares, cruise times, and other information.

SCHADE-MYLANDER PLAZA

(End of Columbus Ave., Sandusky) Some places simply exude a special quality. Schade-Mylander Plaza at the end of Columbus Avenue on Water Street in downtown Sandusky, is one of them. Peaceful, with seating areas looking out on the harbor, and a fountain in the above-freezing weather seasons, this small jewel of a plaza is a favorite spot for photo shoots and family gatherings. Many people spend happy hours sitting here and enjoying the view, the air, the music of the water, the gulls, and the beauty of this place.

WASHINGTON PARK

(County Courthouse, downtown Sandusky) Part of Sandusky's Greenhouse & City Historic Parks program, Washington Park by the **County Courthouse** in downtown Sandusky provides a peaceful and interesting place to stroll and absorb information about the city. A memorial in the park honors fire department officials, the police, and veterans with a creative array of florals and tropical plants. In each quadrant of Washington Park is a floral mound of commemoration.

Also displayed in the park, north of the Courthouse, is Sandusky's landmark **Boy with the Boot**. Commissioned by entrepreneur Voltaire Scott to adorn Scott Park, the Boy was cast by J. W. Fiske Ironworks in New York City. He was moved here from his original resting place in Scott Park after the big tornado of 1924 damaged the park and endangered the Boy. After the park reopened as a parking lot, the Boy was re-installed at Washington Park where he has remained since. Recently, however, the statue was assaulted by vandals, which caused a copy to be made for display in Washington Park. The historic and much revered original Boy is now displayed in safety in **City Hall** on Meigs Street.

SANDUSKY BAY PATHWAY

To continue a walking tour in Sandusky, the Sandusky Bay Pathway is a scenic opportunity. This walkway is designed as a "linear" park built as a recreational trail along Sandusky's waterfront. No motorized vehicles are allowed here. It is designed to be accessible for people with disabilities.

NATURE AND WILDLIFE

Ohio's North Coast is a vast natural resource. Many areas are protected wildlife sanctuaries, while others allow visitors to get up close and personal to wild life and wild places.

SHELDON MARSH STATE NATURE PRESERVE ✪ Must See!

(2715 Cleveland Rd., Huron) In the 1950s a small easterly portion of the Cedar Point peninsula was purchased by a private benefactor, Dr. Shane Sheldon of Sandusky, to secure a bird sanctuary and nature preserve on Sandusky Bay. This tract was acquired by the Ohio Department of Natural Resources in 1979, which combined it with 330 acres of marshland. Today it is a tract totaling 456 acres known as the Sheldon Marsh State Nature Preserve, located in Huron, just a few miles east of **Cedar Point Amusement Park.**

The Sheldon Marsh, protecting vital wetlands, also provides a draw for tourists interested in natural wildlife habitat and its residents. Walking trails curl down to the beachfront. Bird-watching is especially fruitful in this area in the spring and fall, when migratory species are active. Over 300 species of song and shore birds enjoy the protection of Sheldon Marsh. In addition to being a bird sanctuary, the Sheldon Marsh is seen as a place which can provide a shelter for continuation – indeed survival – of a variety of plant and animal species that thrive in this type of wetland habitat. The preserve includes **Monarch Meadow**, a haven for the Monarch Butterfly on its September migration journey south.

LAGOON DEER PARK PETTING ZOO

(1012 Martins Point Rd. (State Rd. 269), Sandusky ☎ 419.684.5701 ☗ sanduskyfunspots.com/deerpark/index.htm) Lagoon Deer Park offers a picnic venue and walking tour to visit various animals kept on-site, including deer and miniature donkeys. There are stocked fishing lagoons for children and their adult companions to go for live catch. This is a rustic area, not modern or upscale. There is an admission charge.

OLD WOMAN CREEK NATIONAL ESTUARINE RESEARCH RESERVE ✪ Must See!

(2514 Cleveland Rd., Huron ☎ 419.433.4601

🖥 oldwomancreek.org) Both a local and national treasure, Old Woman Creek was recognized and established under the Coastal Zone Management Act of 1972. As explained on its Web site, the National Estuarine Research Reserve Systems (NERRS) "is a network of 27 areas representing different biogeographic regions of the United States that are protected for long-term research, water-quality monitoring, education and coastal stewardship." Located between Huron and Vermilion on Cleveland Road (locally known as the Lake Road, old Route 6), Old Woman Creek has the distinction of being the smallest and only freshwater Great Lakes preserve in the National Estuarine Research System.

"Estuarine" means pertaining to estuary, which is a wide-mouth water area of a sea or lake that extends into the mouth of a stream or river. Old Woman Creek's expansion into Lake Erie and the lake's extension into the creek creates the estuarine system. Although Lake Erie is not a saltwater body, it is an inland sea with its own peculiar water ecosystem. The intermingling of the lake's waters with the Old Woman Creek's fresh waters creates a third type of water system different from either the lake or the creek – an estuarine. Its protection and the study area have created a haven for wildlife above and below water at Old Woman Creek.

The NERRS is managed through a partnership between the National Oceanic and Atmospheric Administration (NOAA) and the participating coastal states. As part of the federal statutory research mission, Old Woman Creek houses a complete research lab and weather station. There is a trail system of boardwalks which overlook the wetlands, the creek, the wooded areas, and estuarine habitat. These trails provide excellent photo opportunities for professional and amateur photographers and naturalists and is a peaceful haven for nature lovers and walking enthusiasts. The center also provides guided tours, education seminars, workshops, and even arranges for guest lecturers. A pleasant and staffed visitors' center provides a wealth of information for the public, including natural history exhibits, information about the history of the area, the habitat, a library, and clean restrooms.

Among the natural inhabitants are muskrats, otters, birds, water fowl, and a family of bald eagles who nest on an island within the estuarine. Both mature and adolescent eagles can be sighted by visitors, with close-up views aided by anchored binoculars at the overlook. Benches are provided along the trails for rest and viewing of nature.

The rangers responsible for Old Woman Creek are vigilant. The trails are well maintained for public access and "off limits" areas have been clearly marked. Violations are taken seriously and trespassers venturing into off-limits territory face the risk of being prosecuted.

Old Woman Creek is open daily from dawn to dusk with no admission fee. The Visitor Center is open Monday to Friday during the afternoons from December to March; and Wednesday to Sunday, during the afternoons, from April to November. Check the Web site for dates and other events and programs.

AFRICAN SAFARI WILDLIFE PARK ✪ Must See!
(267 S. Lightner Rd., Port Clinton ☎ 419.732.3606
⬤ africansafariwildlifepark.com) Located approximately 15 miles

west of Sandusky, African Safari is a 100-acre preserve where exotic and endangered animals can be observed from inside a car on a drive-through excursion. Some of the animals encountered on "safari" are camels, elk, warthogs, deer, and zebras. The park provides a bucket of food for those who want to feed the animals during the tour. Since they are used to sightseers with feed buckets, the animals usually are not difficult to find during the drive. The greatest part of the fun for most visitors is seeing one of the animals reach through the car window for a carrot!

There is also a walking tour area called **Safari Junction**, which can be concluded at the **Safari Grill** for a hot dog, choice of sandwich, and soft drink. There are often discount coupons and promotions available plus seasonal rates. Visit the Web site or call for opening times and admission charges.

BLACK SWAMP BIRD OBSERVATORY ✪ Must See!

(Magee Marsh Wildlife Area, 13551 W. State Route 2, Oak Harbor ☎ 419.898.4070 ⬤ bsbobird.org) About 27 miles west of Sandusky lies the Black Swamp Bird Observatory, a marshy region along Lake Erie that provides a migratory habitat for songbirds. This area is a historical remnant of a huge swamp area known to early settlers as "the great terror." The demand for land settlement eventually led to drainage of the once huge and virtually impenetrable swamp land that nearly covered the entire northwest corner of Ohio and a piece of Indiana. This was the Black Swamp and its name has continued today on many places throughout the area.

Several educational and research projects of interest to visitors are ongoing at the Observatory. There are the annual "Big Sits" held in May and in the fall to count sightings of migrating bird species. There is also International Migratory Bird Day in May. Birders host Sunday morning bird walks from the end of April through May and overnight field trips.

Contact the Observatory directly for information about outings, walks, and excursion opportunities. The gift shop is open year-round.

WILLOW POINT WILDLIFE AREA ✪ Must See!

(5200 Wahl Rd., County Rd. 35, Vickery: For information: Wildlife District Two Office, 952 Lima Avenue, Findlay ☎ 419.424.5000) Located seven miles west of Sandusky, the 645-acre Willow Point Wildlife Area is maintained by the Ohio Division of Wildlife. This region supports a widely diverse bird population. Birders may be rewarded with sightings of such elusive feathered species as little blue heron, black tern, yellow-headed blackbird, and short-eared owl. A bald eagle nests in the area. other sightings may include the great blue heron, ducks, Canada geese, black-crowned night heron, swamp sparrow, common yellowthroat, great egret, Caspian tern, common tern, pied-billed grebe, ring-billed, and heron gulls. Spring and fall migratory seasons boost the bird-sighting opportunities.

Willow Point is also presently managed as a public hunting and fishing area. Trappers are permitted to trap raccoon, muskrat, and mink. There is rabbit and game-bird hunting, and fishing on offer as well.

EAST SANDUSKY BAY WATER TRAIL AT BIG ISLAND NATURE PRESERVE ✪ Must See!

(🖱 eriemetroparks.org) In June 2007, Sandusky and the Erie County Metroparks opened the 15-mile East Sandusky Bay

Water Trail at Big Island Nature Preserve. A water trail is called a "blueway" and is designed for people to traverse a trail just as they would through a woodland on foot, except this is done on water by small, hand-powered watercraft such as a kayak, canoe, or small rowboat. The Web site provides a detailed map guide and information sheet for the water trail.

COMMUNITY FOUNDATION PRESERVE AT EAGLE POINT ⊘ Must See!

(3819 Cleveland Rd., also called Lake Rd., old Route 6) Also managed by the Erie County Metroparks, this nature preserve is the home of the American bald eagle, vigorously protected. This lovely 88-acre preserve is located between Sandusky and Huron next to the **Steinen Wildlife Center**. In addition to the eagles, the area is a haven for songbirds and waterfowl. Bird-watchers and photographers are attracted to the opportunities at Eagle Point. The preserve is closed during the eagles' nesting season.

JAMES H. McBRIDE ARBORETUM

(Rye Beach Rd., Huron) The James H. McBride Arboretum provides a serene venue of flowering crabapples in May, and other lovely trees and shrub specimens scattered across 50 acres. This vast expanse include a two-acre lake with a bridge, on the rural campus of **Bowling Green State University's Firelands** branch. The campus is easily found on the west side of Rye Beach Road, about 15 minutes from Sandusky (just south of Route 2 Rye Beach Road exit, across the railroad tracks). Paved walkways make the Arboretum easily accessible.

Other Area Attractions

OTHER ATTRACTIONS

Sandusky offers the enthusiastic visitor an eclectic mix of attractions, from golf courses to caverns.

TRAIN-O-RAMA

**(6732 E. Harbor Rd., Marblehead ☎ 419.734.5856
🖰 trainorama.net)** Train-O-Rama displays an array of model railroads, set up in a wide variety of elaborate themes. Some of the displays include a miniature scaled monorail that skims through detailed miniature theme worlds, such as the amusement park with monorail; a ski-resort; Hillside Drive-in Movie Theater; and airport complete with runway. Train-O-Rama is also a licensed dealer for several model trains, providing a collector's shopping venue as well as entertainment. There is an admission charge to see the model train displays.

SENECA CAVERNS ✪ Must See!

**(15248 Thompson Rd., 178 Bellevue ☎ 419.483.6711
🖰 senecavernsohio.com)** At Seneca Caverns a series of caves descend 110 feet below ground to a crystal clear flowing stream that forms part of the underground water system of this area of Ohio's northern watershed. A guided walking tour, enhanced with electric lights, through these natural caves that are a registered national landmark takes about an hour. Because temperature below ground stays consistently at about 54°F, warm clothing is recommended for the tour even on a hot summer day, as well as comfortable shoes.

For additional fun, Seneca Caverns also operates a water mining sluice for panning for minerals and fossils brought in from around the world. Contact Seneca Caverns for hours and admission rates or check the Web site.

SANDUSKY STATE THEATER ✪ Must See!

(107 Columbus Ave., Sandusky ☎ 419.626.1347) Located in the historic area of downtown Sandusky, the equally historic State Theater is a center for entertainment and the performing arts that has brought in national celebrities and local productions alike, often to sell-out audiences. Its year-round season of shows includes dinner theater productions. The full schedule is accessible on its Web site.

LYMAN HARBOR

(1615 First St., Sandusky ☎ 419.626.6545 🖱 lymanharbor.com) Lyman Harbor has developed a multi-entertainment concept that showcases dining and musical entertainment, combined with a marina. The idea is to have fun at Lyman Harbor even if one does not own a boat. Located on the waterfront in downtown Sandusky, it provides patrons a choice of pub or waterfront dining. It remains closed during the winter. Check out the Web site for what is happening and when, and for how much.

TEAROSE TEAROOM ✪ Must See!

(218 E. Washington St., Sandusky ☎ 419.627.2773) The Tearose Tearoom occupies a historic house that maintains a charming ambience. Tea and lunch include the option of having one's tea leaves read by the hostess. The tearoom is cozy, relaxed, and reasonably priced.

SORROWFUL MOTHER SHRINE ✪ Must See!

**(4106 State Rte. 269, Bellevue ☎ 419.483.6711
📱 sorrowfulmothershrine.com)** Sorrowful Mother Shrine is
a 120-acre place of wooded beauty, augmented with wild-
flowers and planted gardens that seek to provide serenity for
pilgrimage, prayer, peace, worship, or simply personal medi-
tation. In short, the shrine exists for both body and spirit.
It is the oldest Marian shrine of the Midwest, founded in
1850 by Father Francis de Sales Brunner of the Society of
the Most Precious Blood, now called the Missionaries of the
Most Precious Blood. Pathways invite solitary or group walks.
Devotees may follow the outdoor **Stations of the Cross** or
seek the replicas of the **Lourdes and Sepulchre Grottoes.**
The **Stained Glass Memorial Chapel** alone is a small,
awesome work of art.

In addition to the 14 Stations of the Cross and the Grottoes,
there are 39 picnic areas and 38 restrooms on the property,
and even a dog walking area. The **Pilgrim and Information
Center** contains a cafeteria as well.

Though the ambience is spiritual and peaceful, the shrine is
rich in events and activities. Its Web site is a good source to
find out dates of special events, mass times, and pilgrimage
information.

GHOSTLY MANOR THRILL CENTER ✪ Must See!

**(3319 Milan Rd., Route 250, Sandusky ☎ 419.626.4467
📱 ghostlymanor.com)** "Thrill" for the whole family is the theme
of the activities at Ghostly Manor. **Skateworld** is set up for
roller skating and the **XD 3D Theater** for simulated motion
thrill rides. But the centerpiece here is the haunted mansion,

where Ghostly Manor aims to make every moment in the house an adrenaline shock for its hapless visitors. If a person's imagination is up for the thrill of being scared by contrived surprises, a stop at Ghostly Manor should satisfy. Most visitors find the exhibits well done, but judgment should be exercised with very young children for some of these activities. A **Holiday Light Show** with music is presented for the Christmas Holidays, which can be enjoyed from the car.

PREHISTORIC FOREST AND MYSTERY HILL

(P.O. Box 477, 8232 East Harbor Rd., Marblehead
☎ **419.798.5230 🖰 mysteryhill.com)** Take a walk back in time and beyond a magic waterfall to encounter lifelike dinosaurs and mastodon, replicas of their ancestors who once lived in this area. Mystery Hill exhibits its strange forces and challenges visitors to explain why some things, such as water running uphill seem to defy the laws of nature. Whether one figures it out or just enjoys it, it is one of those fun experiences that populate most vacations with giggles and moments of thought. Open from Memorial Day to Labor Day.

ISLAND ADVENTURES

(289 SE Catawba Rd., Rte. 53N, Port Clinton ☎ 419.732.2020
🖰 **island-adventures.net)** Located about 20 minutes west of Sandusky, Island Adventures offers something for adults and children alike. Musical accompaniment with waterfalls, streams, and ponds adorn Island Adventures' miniature golf course. Along with an 18-hole challenge of unique holes, there is the **Vertical Challenge Climbing Wall** and the inside **Arcade.** Children especially seem to enjoy sifting for "gems" in the waterway sluice and then children of all ages head for the

go-cart races of the **Redline Raceway**. This attraction is open seasonally and subject to weather, especially for the outdoor "adventures." Check the schedule on the Web site or call for information specific to your plans.

HURON PLAYHOUSE

(325 Ohio St., The McCormick School Building, Huron
☎ 419.433.4744 ✆ bgsu.edu) Every summer, the Huron Playhouse presents a series of classic, popular theater productions, a division of Bowling Green State University Department of Theater and Film. Check the Web site for what is playing, dates, ticket price, and availability. Just a short drive east of Sandusky, live theater offers a summer entertainment interlude.

LAUREL RUN COOKING SCHOOL

(2600 North Ridge Rd., Vermilion ☎ 440.984.LRCS
✆ laurelruncookingschool.com) Looking for something a little different to do while you are on vacation? "The Cooking School in the Country" at Laurel Run might have something cooking for an afternoon or a night out. A variety of classes are offered throughout the month, some during the day, some in the evening, including private classes, cooking basics, and family-fun nights like "kids and cookies." Some events are set up as demonstrations with dinner. Laurel Run's calendar is usually up on its Web site about three months in advance.

MILLS CREEK GOLF COURSE

(1933 Mills St., Sandusky ☎ 419.627.5803
✆ ci.sandusky.oh.us/recreation/millscreek.htm) Mills Creek is an 18-hole public course right in Sandusky. It is open from mid-March to mid-November.

THUNDERBIRD HILLS GOLF CLUB

(Huron 🕿 thunderbirdhills.com) In Huron, Ohio, approximately ten minutes from Cedar Point, is Thunderbird Hills, a 36-hole public golf course. Nearly 50 years old, it is a mature course with levels achievable for most golfers. A driving range is also available here. Inquire about fees and tee times.

SAWMILL CREEK RESORT

(East of Cedar Point on Cleveland Rd., Route 6 🕿 sawmillcreekresort.com) More than just a hotel, Sawmill Creek Lodge offers a well-regarded 18-hole golf course and marina facilities for fishing and boating, a swimming pool, and tennis courts, as well as its own restaurant and shopping opportunities. The food is always good and the Lake Erie coastline location offers premium ambience. The lodge offers amenities suitable for individuals and families, as well as business conference centers. It is often a venue for weddings. Special weekend and holiday packages are available by reservation. Advance booking is recommended.

SIDNEY FROHMAN PLANETARIUM

(Sandusky Area Supp. Ed. Center, 2130 Hayes Ave., Sandusky 🕿 419.621.2761) Planetariums are up-to-date museums of the sky, offering artificial panorama of the planets, constellations, and the Milky Way as they appear at various times of the year. Open to the public, the Sidney Frohman Planetarium offers various programs for adults and children. Check for events that may be on the schedule as they vary from time to time.

SANDUSKY CULTURAL CENTER

(2130 Hayes Ave., Sandusky ☎ 419.625.1188

📱 sanduskyculturalcenter.org) The Sandusky Cultural Center
provides ongoing art exhibits featuring both local and national
artists, with a focus on diversity and multicultural awareness.
The center partners with local schools for educational enrich-
ment and dedicates an area to showcase the work of local
students in art and writing. Art collections are also showcased
from time to time. Although something is usually going on, the
gallery is only open during exhibitions, so it is wise to check in
advance to make sure exhibits are on display. The center also
organizes artist and community receptions from time to time,
which are announced on the Web site.

MARINAS

Sandusky is on the waterfront and many people find that their
favorite place is floating on Lake Erie. There are numerous marinas in the area offering a wide range of services.

BATTERY PARK MARINA

(701 East Water St., Sandusky ☎ 419.625.6142

📱 batterypark.com) Battery Park is a full-service marina with
fuel dock. The park also offers a pleasant place for strolling
and picnicking, a restaurant, lounge, pool, and tennis courts.
Dockage is available for both transient and seasonal boaters and
several boat storage options. Off-site launch is also available.

CRANBERRY CREEK MARINA

(4319 Cleveland Rd., E., Route 6, Huron ☎ 419.433.3932/ 440.967.3932 ⓦ cranberrycreekmarina.com) Located at Ruggles Beach, Cranberry Creek has a public boat ramp, a bait/tackle shop, seasonal and transient dockage, and just maybe some free advice on where the fish are running.

SADLER SAILING BASIN

(P.O. Box 663, Sandusky ☎ 419.668.3246) Sadler Sailing Basin is a marina for sail boats only, and is open to sailors from I-LYA member clubs. Contact the dock master for information.

SANDUSKY HARBOR MARINA

(1 Huron St., Sandusky ☎ 800.877.3625) Sandusky Harbor Marina provides full marina services with shore amenities to supplement the dockage, plus repair services. There is a security gate and year-round storage options are available.

SANDUSKY YACHT CLUB

(529 E Water St., Sandusky ☎ 419.625.6567 ⓦ sanduskyyachtclub.com) The Yacht Club is located in downtown Sandusky on the bay between the **Battery Park Marina** and **Shoreline Park**. It offers reciprocal membership club affiliations. Check the Web site for details.

SON RISE MARINA

(1535 First St., Sandusky ☎ 419.624.8557/888.508.3625 ⓦ sonrisemarina.com/Welcome/default.asp) Son Rise offers full marina services and storage options.

VENETIAN MARINA

(2035 First St., Sandusky ☎ 800.487.3625

🖱 **hotymarine.com/Venetian%20Marina/Welcome/default.asp)**

Located close to Cedar Point, Venetian Marina offers full service dockage, landside amenities, and winter storage options. It is a fenced-in, gated secure facility.

SANDUSKY BAY FISHING

Lake Erie, and Sandusky Bay in particular, are perennially popular fishing draws. Fishers in Sandusky Bay can find yellow perch, channel catfish, white bass, bullhead, crappie, northern pike, largemouth bass, smallmouth bass, bluegill, steelhead, carp, and freshwater drum. Lake Erie walleye and coho salmon are sometimes taken from the bay as well, though these fish are generally sought farther out on the lake. Persistent fishers may also find dogfish and longnose gar. Steelhead attract anglers to the local rivers, such as the Vermilion River, in mid-winter.

Best catches for smallmouth bass generally run late June, August, and September, usually in the Bass Island areas, Sandusky Bay, and the rocky mainland shorelines. Walleye is happiest as a deep water fish, and generally less abundant in the bay. It can be caught year-round; best times tend to be from early spring through summer. Walleye bait recommended in the summer is crankbait, worms, or spoons. However, for those who want to try their hand at them off the shoreline in the fall and winter, some folks recommend baiting with minnows and shiners.

The best fishing for yellow perch is generally spring and fall in the central and western basin. Check with the local fishing sports for where they are running. The fish do not read the guides or listen to the bait shop talk, and follow their own patterns. Bait recommended is minnows or shiners.

The bullhead fishing generally starts late March and carries through the rest of the year. The best time for crappie in the bay is said to be April, May, and October. The Division of Wildlife reports that while channel catfish and freshwater drum are always to be found, the best time recommended for fishing them in Sandusky Bay is June through September.

Fishing is not restricted to the warmer seasons. Ice fishing is popular on Sandusky Bay, Put-in-Bay, and elsewhere on Lake Erie, mostly for crappies and yellow perch. Up-to-date fishing reports are available online or by telephone. (☎ *888.466.5347/419.625.3187* 🖱 *westernbasinsportfishingassociation.com)*

FISHING LICENSES

For visitors to enjoy fishing in the waters in the area, fishing licenses are mandatory. When you get your fishing license, confirm your bag and size limit for each fish species. These may vary as per the season.

Fishing licenses can be purchased at most bait shops and from the **Ohio Division of Wildlife** *(305 E. Shoreline Dr., Sandusky)*. There are several classes of licenses: resident licenses for Ohio residents of at least six months (age 16–65); annual non-resident; one-day resident or non-resident; three-day non-resident, or seniors.

FISHING CHARTERS

(🖱 **sanduskyfunspots.com)** Fishing charters abound in the Sandusky area and on Lake Erie. These professional services live and breathe Lake Erie fishing and "follow the fish." The charter folks can provide a customized experience for the novice and advance sports enthusiast alike.

WINERIES

Tourists with a taste for the finer things in life will enjoy exploring the wineries in the region. Wine aficionados can sample local wines at two of the recommended wineries.

FIRELANDS WINERY ✪ Must See!
(917 Bardshar Rd., Sandusky ☎ 419.625.5474
🖱 firelandswinery.com) Firelands Winery by name and history reflects the native origins of the Sandusky area. Grapes were one of the earliest cultivated harvests of the area, giving rise to an abundant local wine industry. Firelands Winery is open year-round for tours, wine tasting, and snacks, and also has a fine gift shop. Groups under 15 do not need a reservation for a visit. Alcohol-free juices are part of the winery's fare for children and teetotalers. Look carefully at the label to tell the difference. The winery stays open for a longer time from June through October.

PAPER MOON VINEYARDS
(2008 State Rd., State Route 60, Vermilion ☎ 440.967.2500
🖱 papermoonvineyards.com) Both an attraction and a place to sample wine and a light menu fare, Paper Moon is a new vineyard in Vermilion, a place long known for quality grapes. Paper Moon is now reviving the local tradition. It is located in a country vineyard setting of authentic charm and offers an array of wine selections.

Other Area Attractions

Sandusky Area Accommodations

There are many sights and activities to visit in this Ohio playground besides the great amusement park. Staying outside the park makes travel to other venues easier, and the overall stay more affordable. The Sandusky area also offers other choices of accommodation in the surrounding areas.

Although many of the expected hotel chains are available in the Sandusky area, bed and breakfasts have become favored places to stay and enjoy the local flavor of town and countryside.

Of course, many visitors staying in Sandusky opt to stay in one of the several Cedar Point hotels, which are near the park. For information on these hotels, see the "Cedar Point" chapter.

BED AND BREAKFASTS

Visitors looking for cozy accommodation with all modern amenities can opt to stay in one of the Sandusky area's many bed and breakfasts.

ANGEL WELCOME BED AND BREAKFAST

(2 Front St., Milan ☎ 419.499.0094/866.499.0094) Milan is an all-American small town about 15 minutes south of Sandusky. It is situated on the crossroads of two main highways, Routes 113 and 250, making it very accessible to tourist destinations in all directions.

The Angel Welcome Bed and Breakfast is an 1828 Federal-style house that was originally a private home built not far from **Thomas Edison's Birthplace**. The hosts emphasize comfort and offer tailored programs for special occasions in addition to their standard breakfast options.

COTTAGE ROSE ✪ Must See!

(210 West Adams St., Sandusky ☎ 419.625.1285) Located in downtown Sandusky, Cottage Rose is an English Tudor-style home dating from about 1913. Its owner has furnished the home with antiques, including some of the house's original wallpaper and furniture. It is conveniently located within walking distance of the island ferries, museums, **Washington Park** gardens, theater, restaurants, and antique shopping. Breakfast and ambience is augmented with – what else – an abundance of roses.

WAGNER'S 1844 INN ✪ Must See!

(230 East Washington St., Sandusky ☎ 419.626.1726 ⬟ lrbcg.com/wagnersinn) As many B&Bs strive to do, Wagner's 1844 Inn, listed on the National Register of Historic Places, takes visitors back in time to historic downtown Sandusky. Although preservation of its era is important, Wagner's has not ignored the 21st-century conveniences such as wireless Internet. There is also a billiard room. Breakfast can be enjoyed in the dining room or enclosed courtyard. The local sites of interest in downtown Sandusky are only a few steps away, such as the **Washington Park** gardens and floral displays, **Schade-Mylander Plaza**, **State Theater**, antique shops, **Merry-Go-Round Museum**, **Follet House**, and other attractions of the city center. It is open year-round; inquire for reservations and rooms available to suit personal taste. Online registration is also available.

THE SIMPSON-FLINT HOUSE BED AND BREAKFAST
⭐ Must See!

(234 E. Washington St., Sandusky ☎ 419.621.8679
📶 **bedandbreakfast.com/ohio-sandusky-simpson-flint-house.html)**
Spacious rooms, generous breakfasts, and a pleasant ambience
are the compliments most often heard about The Simpson-
Flint House, a 1890s Queen Anne Victorian period house. It
has the modern conveniences of air conditioning, free long-
distance phone service, and wireless Internet. Its downtown
location is walking distance from the historic features of
Sandusky while still being only a few minutes' drive from the
Cedar Point Parks and other attractions.

1890 QUEEN ANNE BED AND BREAKFAST
(714 Wayne St., Sandusky ☎ 419.626.0391) Located in old
downtown Sandusky, not far from the town square, this
historic house offers a retreat choice of three large rooms,
each with private bath, furnished with antiques, and air conditioned. Guests are served a full breakfast and have access to
the house's patio and garden. Call ahead for reservations and
information.

THE BIG OAK BED & BREAKFAST COUNTRY INN
(2501 S. Campbell St., Sandusky ☎ 419.627.0329
📶 **thebigoakbb.com)** The Big Oak has been reincarnated from
a 1879 farmhouse to an up-to-date 14-room guesthouse
(including air conditioning). Named for the big oak tree in the
yard, The Big Oak provides an outdoor garden setting for its
guests as well as an antique-adorned common room indoors.
Breakfasts are hearty. The ambience is welcoming. Holiday

decorations provide nostalgia. The Big Oak is open year-round except for December 24th and 25th.

CAPTAIN MONTAGUE'S BED AND BREAKFAST
⭐ Must See!

(229 Center St., Huron ☎ 419.433.4756/800.276.4756 🖱 captainmontagues.com) Just a few miles east of Sandusky on the Lake Road is another small Lake Erie town, Huron, situated on the Huron River. It is home to Captain Montague's Bed and Breakfast, which has taken as its theme an "Irish welcome." Once an 1870s manor house, Captain Montague's is a short walk to Huron's Lake Erie beach. The Huron River is also close by, with its own municipal dockage. The owners work to please, from helping visitors find their way to their destinations to making sure they relax and have the peace they may be seeking during their stay. Captain Montague's is known for its cleanliness and friendly atmosphere. Located in a quaint section of small Huron, it is still close to Cedar Point and other area attractions.

RYAN'S CARDINAL HOUSE COTTAGE
(1208 Cleveland Rd. W., Huron ☎ 419.433.3408 🖱 cardinalhousecottage.com) This small B&B offers two bedrooms, one with a queen bed, one with bunk beds, suggesting a quiet hideaway convenient for a family looking for a central location near Lake Erie in a small-town atmosphere. Cedar Point is about a 15-minute drive to the west. Huron's charming beach and local dairy queen are popular nearby features. Advance reservations are required.

GILCHRIST GUESTHOUSE ⭐ Must See!

(5662 Huron St., Vermilion ☎ 440.967.1238) Heading further east from Huron by another 15 minutes or so on the Lake Road brings one to another quaint old fishing village, Vermilion, spanning the Vermilion River. Shaded by mature Ohio buckeye trees, Gilchrist Guesthouse is a stately B&B that sits in the oldest part of Vermilion, a block from the lake. Listed on the National Register, the house dates from circa 1885. Originally the home of Lake Captain J.C. Gilchrist, it is furnished with antiques and welcomes visitors for overnight or longer stays. Kitchen suites are available.

Gilchrist Guesthouse provides a pleasant, secluded easterly anchorage for exploration of greater Sandusky's playground. The house is only a quick walk to the public beach, city docks, Vermilion's charming downtown shopping district, and the famous five-star **Chez Francois** restaurant set on the Vermilion River.

A stroll up Main Street takes visitors to pleasant shops such as **Decidedly Different** – purveyor of gourmet whole and fresh-ground coffees, teas, and one-of-a-kind gifts; **Lee's Landing,** a nautical gift shop; and **Brummer's Chocolates**, a delight of in-store made chocolates, candy, and a unique assortment of cards and gifts. Intersecting Main Street is Liberty Avenue, offering more shops such as an art store, an ice cream parlor, an old-fashioned soda fountain, plus sandwich shops and the public library.

Also within walking distance from Gilchrist are the local Vermilion marinas, bait shop, and marine/camping gear stores.

GEORGIAN MANOR INN ⊙ Must See!

(123 West Main St., Norwalk ☎ 419.663.8132/800.668.1644
📟 georgianmanorinn.com) Norwalk is the county seat of
adjoining Huron County, and just a quick drive south of
Sandusky on State Route 250. The Georgian Manor Inn is an
award-winning 9,000-square foot Georgian Revival mansion
home converted to a luxury bed-and-breakfast getaway.
Furnished with antiques and fine art and surrounded with
classic well-tended gardens, the inn could easily be classified as
a tourist attraction in and of itself.

THE VICTORIAN INN BED & BREAKFAST

(5622 East Harbor Rd., Marblehead ☎ 800.501.3791
📟 victorianinnbb.com) Located west of Sandusky on the
Marblehead peninsula, The Victorian Inn Bed & Breakfast was
originally a home built in 1866. Remodeled in 2008, the house's
location is in close proximity to most of the attractions of the
area – from Sandusky to Put-in-Bay, and Kelleys Island ferries
and of course the **Marblehead Lighthouse**. Rooms are air
conditioned with TVs and wireless Internet. The rooms are
originally appointed, one unusually done with a mural vista of
the Marblehead Lighthouse and Lake Erie. There is an outside
deck for relaxing as well. Whole house rates are available.

WATER PARK THEME RESORTS

For guests who cannot get enough of splashing around in the
water, the area also offers accommodations with a water park
theme. Staying at a water park resort usually involves a more
resort-like experience, with additional attractions, restaurants,
and shops on the premises.

GREAT WOLF LODGE

(4600 Milan Rd., Route 250, Sandusky ☎ 866.679.9731
📱 greatwolf.com) Great Wolf Lodge has become a popular getaway for families who come to enjoy its year-round indoor water park and suite-style accommodations. More than just a hotel, it is a self-enclosed theme water park, one of a chain of the Great Wolf Resorts located throughout the United States and Canada. Its water park is open only to registered guests. Located on Route 250 in Sandusky, it is easily accessible from Route 2.

Certain suites are set up to intrigue and attract families, an example being the "wolf den" suite, which includes a cave theme enclosure in the room with a bunk bed for the kids including their own TV, separate from the adults' queen bed and sleep sofa (and their own TV). There is also a Great Wolf's "KidCabin" suite option; this arrangement contains a "log cabin" within the suite for the kids. There are standard hotel rooms and suite options with fireplaces available as well. All rooms have free wireless Internet, a coffeemaker, and other amenities. It is best to inquire directly to discuss room preference, rates, and availability.

KALAHARI WATERPARK RESORT AND KAHUNAVILLE

(7000 Kalahari Drive, Sandusky ☎ 877.525.2527
📱 kalahariresorts.com/oh) Located south of Sandusky, off Route 250, Kalahari is another indoor theme water park and hotel. Despite some minor complaints that the Kahunaville restaurant price of food is high for the quality and that some of the water activities are not always open due to short staffing, many patrons keep returning for second and

third visits. Cleanliness of the rooms consistently gets high marks. The hotel suites are designed on African themes – for example, the Hut and Desert Suites accommodate four people. Kalahari frequently runs promotions, coupons, and specials, plus holiday activities such as an Easter Egg hunt. It is easily accessible from both Ohio Route 2 and the Ohio Turnpike.

QUALITY INN & SUITES RAINWATER PARK

(1935 Cleveland Rd., Sandusky ☎ 419.626.6761/800.654.3364 ⬤ qualityinn.com/hotel-sandusky-ohio-OH279) Rain Quality Inn offers a small water park venue close to Cedar Point, with fair-sized updated rooms, free high-speed Internet access, and continental breakfast included. Some of the rooms offer a whirlpool. The hotel is part of a family water park plus laser tag, an arcade, and bowling alley. In addition, there is off-track horse race gambling for the adults, and food on the premises.

OTHER ACCOMMODATIONS

Apart from bed and breakfasts, tourists can stay in other lodgings including cottages that afford privacy, lakeside rooms with wonderful views, or even a resort with all the trappings necessary for a luxurious stay.

LAKESIDE ASSOCIATION

(Marblehead Peninsula ⬤ lakesideohio.com) Located on Lake Erie's shore on the Marblehead Peninsula west of Sandusky, Lakeside is its own vacation community of cottages (available for rental) and host to a cornucopia of recreational activities. It has its own beach front, picnic areas, shopping, and events.

Known as the "Chautauqua on Lake Erie," Lakeside is a picturesque, defined community steeped in a history of spiritual retreat and religious Christian orientation of Methodist origin that lives on today in a spirit of community wholeness. Lakeside hosts ongoing social, educational, and artistic events throughout the summer and holiday seasons.

EVENING SONG COTTAGE

(310 Walnut Ave., Lakeside ☎ 419.732.6700

☗ eveningsongcottage-bb.com) Evening Song Cottage is a more remote B&B getaway, with six air-conditioned guest rooms in historic Lakeside Community.

KEYSTONE GUEST HOUSE

(202 Maple Ave., Lakeside ☎ 614.204.6203/419.798.4263

☗ keystoneguesthouse.net) Keystone also is located in Lakeside and offers both rooms and efficiencies furnished in period style. Rooms can be viewed on their Web site.

SOUTH BEACH RESORT

(8620 East Bayshore Rd., Marblehead ☎ 419.788.4900

☗ sbresort.com) Hotel, cottages, and a marina are put together at South Beach on the coast of Sandusky Bay in scenic Marblehead, west of Sandusky. Included in offered amenities are spa services of Swedish or hot stone massage and facials. Although South Beach caters to boaters and fishing, there are pools, a sundeck, and playground for the kids as well. So if half the family is not into fishing, there are many other activities to keep them happy and occupied. The resort's Web site provides guidance for costs and types of accommodations.

SAWMILL CREEK RESORT

(400 Sawmill Creek Dr., Huron ⬮ sawmillcreekresort.com) More than just a hotel, Sawmill Creek Lodge occupies 235 acres of golf course, marinas, parking, shops, restaurant, pool, tennis courts, convention center, and hotel. It is located east of Cedar Point, off the Lake Road. Special weekend and holiday packages are available by reservation. Advance booking is recommended.

Dining

The Sandusky area offers a broad range of interesting and unique dining choices, ranging from formal to casual, and gourmet to down-home country style. Listed here are many restaurants and eateries, most in the moderate price range. A few are pricey though. Most will go out of their way to satisfy special dietary requests. Visitors will find it easy to find menu and pricing information on the restaurant Web sites or by telephone inquiry.

ANGRY TROUT

(505 E. Bayview Dr., Sandusky ☎ 419.684.5900) Angry Trout is recommended for people who like fish and seafood. The sauces for some of the dishes have earned mixed reviews; the soups though, fare better. It offers a nice view and casual atmosphere and is within easy walking distance of downtown sights. A kids' menu is included.

BACI NITECLUB AND DINING ✪ Must See!

(5909 Milan Rd., Sandusky ☎ 419.624.9900) Baci provides an upscale, continental ambience and menu that aims to consistently please its patrons. This is a good selection for a night out for dinner. Be sure to try the rack of lamb and lobster.

BAY HARBOR INN

(1 Cedar Point Dr., Sandusky ☎ 419.625.6373) The Bay Harbor Inn earned its reputation years ago for steak and seafood, as well as for its spectacular view of the water. It remains one of Sandusky's best restaurants and is open year-round despite its Cedar Point venue. The restaurant also has a full bar.

Dining

BERARDI'S

(1019 W Perkins Ave., Sandusky ☎ 419.626.4592) Berardi's is a long-time popular, casual family restaurant in Sandusky for "down-home" cooking; it has a second equally popular location on Route 6 in Huron. Don't forget to ask about the homemade pies for dessert. Berardi's is open for breakfast, lunch, and dinner.

BIG BOPPER'S ✪ Must See!

(7581 East Harbor Rd., Route 163 E., Marblehead ☎ 419.734.4458 ◉ bigboppers.net) For a bottomless cup of coffee, hot hot chili, and the latest scoop on local fishing, visitors might not want to miss a stop at Big Bopper's. There is more on the menu to try besides the chili. The restaurant is open for breakfast, lunch, and dinner, and offers coupons on the Web site.

CAMEO PIZZA ✪ Must See!

(702 W Monroe St., Sandusky ☎ 419.626.0187) Cameo Pizza is a full service eat-in or take-out family-owned pizza restaurant with a full-service bar. Sports TVs and a casual family atmosphere make this place warm and inviting. The atmosphere heats up on Ohio State/Michigan Football Game day – the owners' family of several generations gather to cheer both teams in friendly but noisy rivalry on Game Day and all are welcome to join in! The pizza recipe has been a family secret for generations, and part of this recipe is good service.

CASA REAL

(3307 Milan Rd., Route 250, Sandusky ☎ 419.609.9225 ◉ allmenus.com/menus/93391/Casa-Real-Mexican-Restaurant) Mexican fare is the menu at Casa Real. A family-friendly restaurant, it is open for lunch and dinner. The menu can be viewed online.

CHET & MATT'S PIZZA

(1013 E Strub Rd., Sandusky ☎ 419.626.6000
☻ chetmattspizza.com) Chet & Matt's is not just any pizza place. The restaurant is popular for originality, including its peanut butter and jelly dessert pizza and artichoke pizza. This is a place that tends to receive either great or opposite reviews; it all depends on what a person likes in pizza. A good place for families who like variety and are open to trying new things.

CHEZ FRANCOIS ✪ Must See!

(555 N. Main St., Vermilion ☎ 440.967.0630
☻ chezfrancois.com) Chez Francois is located in an historical building with dockage on the Vermilion River. It was once a boat repair shop and ferry dock for the river ferry crossing. After the Vermilion Lagoons were developed, and a main bridge was built further upriver, the ferry crossing became obsolete and the piece of Ferry Street down to the river eventually became a grassy verge. The boat building passed through various uses, including that of being the town's laundry facilities, before it was developed into a restaurant in the 1970s, with dentist offices upstairs. Today, the whole building is occupied by the restaurant.

French cuisine, fine wines, and a long-established reputation for excellence mark this restaurant's cachet. It is also one of the more expensive options, although special menu dinner options and wine-tasting events are often scheduled. From Sandusky, visitors may take a leisurely drive along Lake Erie or travel by boat and dock at one of the restaurant's slips on the river. Men are required to wear a jacket for inside seating, but more casual

Dining

attire is the rule for the deck on the river. Watch the river traffic and the Lake Erie sunsets while enjoying some of the best food on the North Coast. Check out the Web site for what is on offer. Unless one is very lucky, advance reservations are required. The restaurant remains closed in January and February.

CULINARY VEGETABLE INSTITUTE ✪ Must See!

(12304 State Route 13, Milan ☎ 419.499.7500
☗ culinaryvegetableinstitute.com) The Culinary Vegetable Institute has put together top chefs with the freshest local, home-grown organic food to produce delightful gourmet results. Tucked away back in the woods in a private remote setting, everything from table to garnish is clearly done with attention to detail. Special dinners are scheduled at the institute. It offers a cooking class series that may entice a vacation plan. Or, one of its night-out specials may be the pièce de rèsistance of a vacation getaway. The institute would doubtless be pleased to simply give a tour if time permits. The prices here are more upscale.

DALY'S IRISH PUB

(104 Columbus Ave., Sandusky ☎ 419.625.0748) Open for lunch and dinner, Daly's often spices its pub fare with live music. It is best to call for information about the menu and entertainment schedules as these tend to vary.

DAMON'S

(701 E. Water St., Sandusky ☎ 419.627.2424) Located near downtown at **Battery Park**, Damon's is famous for its outstanding BBQ ribs. Dining is casual on the waterfront.

There are other good items on the menu, but it is the ribs that have put this restaurant on the map, and with good reason.

FAMOUS DAVE'S

(1 Cedar Point Drive, Sandusky) Dave's is one of the BBQ chains and located at Cedar Point. It lives up to its reputation for great BBQ ribs and with its location, the restaurant is popular with visitors to the Parks.

MARCONI'S ITALIAN RESTAURANT

(424 Berlin Rd., Huron ☎ 419.433.4341 🖰 marconisitalian.com) Marconi's has been a fixture in the area for decades. Dining and service in the Italian tradition has been the hallmark of Marconi's. A virtual tour of the restaurant and its menu and wine list are available on its Web site.

MARKLEY'S RESTAURANT

(160 Wayne St., Sandusky ☎ 419.627.9441) Markley's is a 50s era diner with traditional American food and service. This place is recommended for breakfast.

MON AMI RESTAURANT AND HISTORIC WINERY
⭐ Must See!

(3845 Wine Cellar Rd., Catawba Island, Port Clinton ☎ 419.787.4445 🖰 monamiwinery.com) Catawba Island is really a peninsula jutting off the mainland by Port Clinton, west of Sandusky. Follow Route 53 north and visitors will find Wine Cellar Road and Mon Ami's sign on the left. Mon Ami offers a great menu and of course, a wide wine selection within the ambience of its historic stone building and gardens. Visit the Web site for a view of the menu and wine list and for the schedule of live entertainment.

NEW SANDUSKY FISH COMPANY

(235 E. Shoreline Dr., Sandusky ☎ 419.621.8263) This eatery offers sandwiches and seafood for takeout only, and specializes in fresh walleye and perch. Walk to the waterside to eat the take-out sandwiches or buy fish to take home.

NICK'S ROADHOUSE

(124 Buckeye Blvd., Port Clinton ☎ 419.732.3069
⬤ **nicksroadhouse.com)** Sports bar, patio, nightclub entertainment, and restaurant bar food are all rolled up into one noisy, tasty package at Nick's Roadhouse. Information and entertainment schedule are usually up-to-date on the Web site.

THE PIT RESTAURANT ✪ Must See!

(3909 Liberty Ave., Route 6, Vermilion ☎ 440.967.7919) This plain, small, quaint little restaurant is clean and friendly. Do not let the unassuming exterior put you off. The Pit's BBQ ribs are, in a word — awesome; the rest of the menu is pretty good too.

SALVATORE'S RISTORANTE ✪ Must See!

(4560 Liberty Ave., Route 6, Suite C, Vermilion ☎ 440.967.0777)
A local favorite, Salvatore's Ristorante is tucked into a small niche with two-room casual dining cast in low lighting (Venetian glass chandeliers) with booths, intimate tables, and full bar. Italian music plays softly in the background and friendly service makes guests feel welcome. The all-Italian menu serves up good, home-cooked Italian dishes that are complimented with hot bread, soups, and salads. Call ahead for hours of service.

Dining

WINDJAMMER RESTAURANT & SCHOONER'S SPORTS BAR

(8037 E. Harbor Rd., Marblehead ☎ 419.798.5677 ● windjammers.biz) A full dinner menu for casual dining, plus appetizers, wings, and more for its late-night menu to go with serious darts playing is on offer at this restaurant. For more information on darts and updated menu, hours, and pricing, visit the Web site.

ZINC BRASSERIE ✪ Must See!

(142 Columbus Ave., Sandusky ☎ 419.502.9462) This is a consistently highly rated little restaurant with fine gourmet food, full bar, and a wide selection of wines. One recent out-of-state visitor described her experience as "outstanding." Repeated visits have proved the consistency and excellent service of this restaurant. Open for lunch and dinner, the restaurant's live guitar music provides entertainment and background for evenings.

South Bass is the most populated of the three Bass Islands.

Bass Islands

───────────────────────────────────────●

Offshore from Sandusky lie three islands called South Bass, Middle Bass, and North Bass. The most populated and developed of the three today is South Bass Island, home to the town of Put-in-Bay, Ohio.

Middle Bass Island is less populated and commercial by comparison to South Bass Island. The principal industry of Middle Bass historically has been vineyards and wine making. Most notable in Middle Bass Island was the **Lonz Winery**. The main ferry connection from the mainland to Middle Bass is the **Miller Ferry**. The **Sonny-S Ferry** runs between Put-in-Bay and Middle Bass. There is also an air strip here. North Bass Island is not commercially developed and has only a few private residents.

SOUTH BASS ISLAND – PUT-IN-BAY

As a passenger on the **Jet Express** ferry headed for Put-in-Bay, a look at fellow passengers will provide a sense of the broad range of attractions the island holds for people. On a typical morning there is the young couple with their backpacks and bicycles; a honeymoon couple staying at the Resort; the young families with strollers and kids of stair-step ages; the bearded man with glasses on a chain reading a book about submerged Lake Erie shipwrecks; the middle-aged couple checking for their sunscreen talking about meeting relatives who live on the island; an Ohio State college student who is going to be spending time on a research project on Gibraltar Island; another college student who works at one of the restaurants for the summer. Some of the people are headed out for the day. Others plan to be there for several days or longer. Some live on the island.

Bass Islands

South Bass is the third largest of the Lake Erie Islands, behind Pelee, the largest (part of Canada) and Kelleys Island, the second largest. Though it has its year-round residents, its own school, and town government, just like any other Ohio town, the population of Put-in-Bay multiplies exponentially in the summer season. As signaled with the **Blessing of the Fleet**, the tourist season opens and with it the sleeping businesses, hotels, and bed and breakfasts, mostly closed for the winter, open to receive vacationers, boaters, and partiers. Put-in-Bay is beautiful and fun. It is an island "get away." It is party central.

It is, however, also much more than that. Like Sandusky on the mainland, Put-in-Bay has its place in history. Commodore Oliver Hazard Perry lay his ships at harbor at Put-in-Bay, waiting for the British navy in the War of 1812, and won a decisive battle. Today **Perry's Monument** stands in tall testament to the battle and is a popular draw for visitors to the island.

AREA HISTORY

South Bass Island, including Put-in-Bay, was designated as "Island No. One" or "Bass Island" in the Connecticut Land Grant of the Western Reserve. It was first drawn by Pierpont Edwards, who paid a sum of $26,087 for it and the other islands. It is reported that thereafter these islands, with Put-in-Bay, were deeded, starting with a Huron County sheriff's sale through a series of transactions to Eli Whitney, son of the inventor, as a marriage settlement trust in 1853. In 1854, Eli Whitney and his wife sold them to one J. Rivera St. Jurgo, more commonly called de Rivera, for $44,000. He fell in love with the island at first sight and bought all of the islands from the Whitneys within 48 hours.

De Rivera, whose primary home was in New York, made Put-in-Bay his summer home and first established a sheep ranch there. From that enterprise he moved on to a fruit farm. He also tested the ground and found it suitable for vineyards. De Rivera gradually sold off land on the island to others who had interests in summering there – he sold **Gibraltar Island**, which sits just off South Bass, to Sandusky financier Jay Cooke. Eventually, de Rivera lost all his holdings in financial ruin and his remaining holdings on Put-in-Bay went to creditors.

Gibraltar Island, once owned for decades by Sandusky scion Jay Cooke, is a small island lying close off Put-in-Bay. The island serves as a natural shelter for Put-in-Bay's harbor. Cooke paid de Rivera $3,000 for the island and made it his retreat and place for entertaining friends and family. In 1925 a wealthy Columbus, Ohio, businessman named Julius Stone purchased Gibraltar Island from the Cooke family. Stone donated it to Ohio State University. The Ohio State connection remains to this day, for Gibraltar Island is now a naturalist research and education center.

Another famous connection of historical note in Put-in-Bay that should not pass without mention is its early resident, John Brown, Jr.; his father was the famous abolitionist John Brown who was executed for his ill-fated raid on Harper's Ferry in 1859. John Sr. had trained a group of men, including his sons Owen, Oliver, and Watson, to raid the federal armory at Harper's Ferry, Virginia, as a protest against slavery. John Brown Sr.'s plan was to seize the ammunitions at the armory without bloodshed. The plan went badly; townspeople were aroused and battle ensued. People were killed, including

Brown's sons, except Owen, who escaped with four others. Brown Sr. stood trial for treason and was hung. His death, the trials, and executions of others involved, served to raise the battle cry of pro-abolitionists in the north, including the core group of abolitionists in northern Ohio.

Thus, John Brown, Jr.'s presence in Put-in-Bay was that of a quiet, but revered figure in an area heavily committed to the Union cause and the anti-slavery movement. He bought ten acres of land on Put-in-Bay in 1862, when illness forced his retirement from the Union Army, and he lived there with his family until his death in 1895. He and his wife, Wealthy Brown, who died in 1911, are both buried on Put-in-Bay.

Owen eventually escaped to Put-in-Bay with the huge price of $25,000 on his head, following his father's execution. The island was still a quiet, out-of-the-way place in those days and unlike Cedar Point, not yet well known as a resort. Its remoteness in an area of Union sympathizers made it an ideal safe haven. Owen served as a caretaker for Jay Cooke's place on Gibraltar Island for years. He later moved to California in the 1880s.

By the late 19th and early 20th centuries, Put-in-Bay was competing with Cedar Point as a vacation spot. The steamers, *Put-in-Bay* and *G.A. Boeckling* carried passengers between Sandusky, Put-in-Bay, and Detroit. The Hotel Victory opened with fanfare on Put-in-Bay on the 4th of July in 1892. It boasted 625 guest rooms, a dining room that could seat 1,000, and a co-ed swimming pool – an avant garde first in the country. It was also advertised as the largest resort hotel in America. The hotel burned down in 1919.

GETTING AROUND PUT-IN-BAY

Most of the attractions on Put-in-Bay are within walking distance, and a bit of hiking around to see the beauty of the place is part of the fun. For a day trip, visitors have the choice of walking or renting golf carts, bicycles, or mopeds from one of the several rental places available. Many people bring along their own bicycles. Tourists who decide to spend a few days in Put-in-Bay have several lodging options to choose from, including cozy bed and breakfasts and luxury hotels.

GOLF CART RENTALS

(⊕ putinbayrentals.com/secure/cartrental.php) Those staying on island for a few days usually prefer to rent a golf cart to assist with transporting luggage to a hotel or B&B and for getting around the island. Some people even bring over their own car on the **Miller Ferry**. Even with this option, people quickly find that it is still more fun and much easier to rent a golf cart to tool around on the island. Parking is at a premium downtown (even for golf carts). Other than needing a car for getting to and from the ferry, there is not much use for a car for many of the activities on Put-in-Bay.

FISHING CHARTERS

Put-in-Bay is a great jumping-off place for fishing. Two fishing charters available out of Put-in-Bay are **Hard Water Charters** (☎ *419.285.3106* ⊕ *hardwatercharters.com*) and **Chrysler Marine** (☎ *419.285.4631* ⊕ *patchryslermarine.com*).

ATTRACTIONS

Tourists who can break away from the amusement park will definitely not be disappointed on a visit to the region. There are a variety of things to see and do on a visit to Put-in-Bay.

DiRIVERA PARK

Put-in-Bay's beautiful downtown park is the central open space of the town and the first thing one sees as the boat pulls in the harbor. It is a pleasant place to relax and rest after shopping, to have a picnic lunch, let the kids run and play, or take a nap in the shade. The views of the harbor and lake are gorgeous, especially at sunset. Public restrooms and showers are available.

AQUATIC VISITORS CENTER

(1 Peach Point Rd.) The live fish displays and hands-on exhibits of Aquatic Visitors Center are some of the attractions for both kids and adults. There is a playroom and an opportunity for children to try their hand at fishing. The center is open to the public from late May to September. Admission is free.

PERRY'S CAVE

(979 Catawba Ave.) South Bass Island is known to be underscored with caves. Accessed at 979 Catawba Avenue (1/2 mile from downtown Put-in-Bay) Perry's Cave, an Ohio Natural Landmark, is a limestone cave approximately 52 feet underground, said to have been discovered by Commodore Perry. It measures 208 feet by 165 feet and is richly decorated in stalactites, stalagmites, and cave pearls, all well-explained by the cave guides in the 20-minute tours conducted several times a day. An underground lake is also associated with the cave.

The temperature below stays at about 50°F year-round, so one should dress accordingly for the tour with a sweater and easy walking shoes. An **Antique Care Museum, Butterfly Museum,** and **War of 18 Holes Miniature Golf** are also located at the site of Perry's Cave.

GIBRALTAR ISLAND AT PUT-IN-BAY
(OSU Stone Lab ☎ 419.285.1800

▉ **stonelab.osu.edu or twitter@stonelab)** Still owned by Ohio State University, Gibraltar Island is home to a full-time laboratory and research center, part of the Ohio Sea Grant College Program. The **Franz Theodore Stone Laboratory** is located here. The island is slightly more than a stone's throw off Put-in-Bay, but just far off enough to require a water taxi to reach. Tours have been made available to the public at a modest cost (plus the cost of the water taxi) to provide information about Gibraltar Island's history, a view of **Cooke Castle's** exterior, and explanation of the ongoing research at the lab. It is an interesting tour and allows a view of Put-in-Bay from an historical perspective that is otherwise not available. Ohio's Sea Grant Program is one of 30 such programs dedicated to Great Lakes marine resources. Ohio State University also owns the **South Bass Island Lighthouse** on Gibraltar Island and offers tours at certain times. Information is available at the Stone Lab.

ISLAND TOUR TRAIN
The Island Tour Train takes visitors on an open-air tour around the island. It departs from its downtown depot at the corner of Delaware and Toledo Avenue, near the ferry dock. When disembarking from the ferry boats, the train is readily visible. This is a great way to get an introduction to the island.

Bass Islands

KAYAK THE BAY

"Just like riding a bicycle," the kayaks offer single or double options for taking a water tour in the bay or around the island. This service is located at Bay View Avenue Crew's Nest Dock B.

KIMBERLY'S CAROUSEL

Children and adults who are kids at heart can seldom resist a merry-go-round and the music will inevitably draw them in to Kimberly's Carousel downtown on Delaware Avenue. The merry-go-round is a 1917 Herschel that gives several animal options to ride, including Pete the Perch. Tickets are purchased at the nearby **Carriage House** souvenir shop.

HEINEMAN'S WINERY ✪ Must See!

(978 Catawba Ave. ☎ 419.285.2811 🖱 heinemanswinery.com) A tradition on South Bass Island, Heineman's Winery offers the opportunity for wine tasting and a lovely hour or two (or more) in its garden with a bottle of wine or non-alcoholic grape juice – whichever is the preferred recipe for rest and relaxation. Plates of cheese and crackers are available to accompany one's grape beverage. The winery is an easy walk from downtown and an afternoon in its garden is a delightful, peaceful way to relax and unwind. Also on offer is a tour of the beautiful **Crystal Cave** and a presentation on the history of wine making, which has been Heineman's business for over 100 years.

LAKE ERIE ISLANDS HISTORICAL SOCIETY MUSEUM

(441 Catawba Ave. ☎ 419.285.2804 🖱 leihs.org) The LEIHS has collected a wealth of information on the early history of the island and its settlers. One of its active projects is a genealogical study and history of the island's residents. It has a database of 14,000 residents, their ancestors and descendants, including summer cottage residents. The museum is actively working on expanding its collection of old photos and oral history of people and events relating to the island. It has a store which does not offer a lot of items, but the ones it has make for wonderful lasting souvenirs of a visit to Put-in-Bay.

PERRY VICTORY AND INTERNATIONAL PEACE MEMORIAL

(☎ 419.285.2184 📞 nps.gov/pevi/index.htm) This tall monument is visible from everywhere on the island. It commemorates not just Oliver Hazard Perry's naval battle in the War of 1812, but a great concept of the long-lasting peace among the U.S., Canada, and the United Kingdom. It is 47 feet taller than the Statue of Liberty and is the only memorial to international peace in the U.S. International park system.

PUT-IN-BAY PARASAIL

(Boardwalk Dock in downtown Put-in-Bay ☎ 419.285.3703 📞 putinbayparasail.com) The Parasail service promises that no experience is required and lots of fun is guaranteed by Captain Jay for ages "3 to 83."

PUT-IN-BAY RACEWAY

(Delaware Ave. ☎ 419.285.2026) "Children" of all ages can enjoy a remote control car-racing competition on this 1:10 scale oval, banked track located on Delaware Avenue, across the street from Put-in-Bay's Chamber of Commerce. Do not underestimate the speed of these little cars. Participants can challenge up to four other racers for a 2.5-minute race.

TAILFINS AMUSEMENT PARK

(tailfnspark.com) Tailfins offers a variety of water activities for the entire family, including bumper boats, remote-controlled boats, arcade, water wars, and virtual bowling. Check the Web site for information on the full range of activities.

BED AND BREAKFASTS

Visit the Web sites of the accommodations listed below for more information, details about rates, and to view photographs of the rooms. Recommended below are some bed and breakfasts that offer comfort and quiet in cozy surroundings.

ARBOR INN BED & BREAKFAST

(511 Trenton Ave., P.O. Box 607 ☎ 419.285.2306
arborinnpib.com) Emphasis here is on quiet ambience in four rooms with king-size beds, central air conditioning, and satellite TV.

ASHLEY'S ISLAND HOUSE

(557 Catawba Ave., P.O. Box 395 ☎ 419.285.2844
ashleysislandhouse.com) Ashley's Island House offers 12 rooms, some with shared baths. The house is close to many of the town's summer attractions and could be a good choice for a large family. The rooms are prettily furnished.

GETAWAY INN BED AND BREAKFAST

(210 Concord Avenue, P.O. Box 548 ☎ 419.285.9012
getawayinn.com) The Getaway Inn offers six air-conditioned rooms with private baths. The rooms are not fancy but they are furnished with a sense of charm and comfort.

NIAGARA GUEST HOUSE B&B

(681 Langram Rd., also called Airport Rd., P.O. Box 28
☎ 419.285.7447 🖱 niagaraguesthouse.com) Named for
Commodore Perry's Flagship, the Niagara offers four large
rooms for couples only; rooms are air conditioned with
private baths. More information is available on its Web site.
Reservations over the telephone are made between 8:00 a.m.
and 10:00 p.m.

EDGEWATER HOTEL

(Delaware Ave., Main downtown ☎ 419.285.2724 April 1–Oct
31; 419.351.5166 Nov 1–April 1 🖱 putinbayrentals.com) The
Edgewater Hotel has location, location, location – very nearly
in the center of the main street of Put-in-Bay. Suites at the
Edgewater Hotel are not fancy but are outfitted with kitchen-
ettes, TV, and air conditioning. Check into reservation requirements and weekend deals. The owners welcome questions.

ENGLISH PINES BED AND BREAKFAST

(182 Concord Ave. ☎ 419.285.2521 🖱 englishpines.com) An
historic home, English Pines offers location, comfort, and
sumptuous breakfasts. With a shaded porch and patios, the
rambling house is the kind of peaceful haven that defines
Put-in-Bay. The Conference Center, shops, winery, restaurants,
and downtown action are close by.

JEANNE'S BED AND BREAKFAST

(745 Langram Rd., P.O. Box 215 ☎ 419.285.8353
🖱 pibsuites.com/jeanne.html) In this B&B, the owner herself
welcomes you into her own home which features three air-
conditioned bedrooms each with its own queen-size bed and a
second twin bed.

LINDA'S BED AND BREAKFAST

(480 Mitchell Rd., P.O. Box 335 ☎ 419.285.3045
☎ lindasbedandbreakfast.com)** This quiet B&B is a private home with two upstairs rooms separated for guests. Couples only are preferred due to the size of the accommodations.

THE VINEYARD BED AND BREAKFAST

(☎ 419.285.6181 ☎ vineyardohio.homestead.com) The Vineyard is an old farmhouse reincarnated as a bed and breakfast. Furnished with antiques, it is set on 20 acres that include a private beach and vineyard.

WISTERIA INN BED AND BREAKFAST

(Langram Rd. between Miller Boat Line and the Downtown ☎ 419.285.2828) This brick home offers rooms for couples only. Its front porch provides a pleasant view of the lake and gardens. Call to get more information about the accommodation.

PARK HOTEL

(☎ 419.285.3581 ☎ parkhotelpib.com) This Victorian era building is a hotel on the main street of Put-in-Bay, next to the famous **Roundhouse Bar**. Rooms do not have private baths but are climate controlled and have overhead fans. Rates and photos are available on the Web site or one can call directly for specific information.

PEACE AND QUIET

(☎ 216.898.9951/216.898.1105) Reservations through Island Club Rentals can be made for these duplex side-by-side effi-ciencies that can be rented together or separately. Each side has its own kitchen, dining area, bathroom, air conditioning, bedroom with two queen beds, and a sleeper sofa. Linens are included. Remotely located, yet not far from Put-in-Bay's downtown party central, these are private accommodations with more privacy than a busy hotel.

THE COMMODORE RESORT

(☎ 419.285.3101 ⬤ commodoreresort.com) Also close to the action, the Commodore Resort is a resort hotel complete with pool, restaurant, bar, and room amenities. Upgraded as of 2008, the Commodore has expanded its rooms, added a Subway shop, and connected **Mr. Ed's Bar and Grille** to its hotel. Reservations can be made online.

CAMPGROUNDS

For tourists interested in getting back to nature and enjoying the outdoors, camping in comfort can also be accommodated at Put-in-Bay.

FOX'S DEN CAMPGROUND

(Langram Rd. ☎ 419.285.5001) This privately owned campground provides both full-service sites and locations for primitive tent camping with restroom and shower facilities available.

SOUTH BASS ISLAND STATE PARK

(Catawba Ave. ☎ 419.285.2112

⬤ ohiodnr.com/parks/lakeerie/tabid/753/Default.aspx) This is a family campground with ten full-service campsites and 125 non-electric sites. There are also four cabents (cabin-tent combination) and one cabin that can be rented by the week through a lottery system.

LUXURY HOTELS

If visitors to the region are willing to loosen their purse-strings for upscale accommodation, Put-in-Bay has some elegant lodgings available as well.

THE PUT-IN-BAY RESORT

(439 Lorain Ave., P.O. Box 267 ☎ 888.742.7829) This is Put-in-Bay's luxury hotel, with the upscale amenities that go with first-class expectations and well-appointed rooms. The hotel has its own pool, complete with Tiki bar. The hotel also has a restaurant – the **Blue Marlin Grill**, a large Jacuzzi, and many organized social activities. These amenities qualify the resort as an attraction in its own right, beyond just being a place to hang one's hat for the night.

THE ISLAND CLUB

(☎ 216.898.9951 🖱 islandclub.com) Contact The Island Club to arrange a stay in a three-bedroom private rental home as opposed to a hotel.

SHOPPING

Shopping on Put-in-Bay is replete with many typical tourist items, but there are unusual and special finds to surprise and delight as well.

AIRBORNE DESIGNS

(Catawba Ave. ☎ 419.285.3333) Next door to the Put-in-Bay Brewing Company, Airborne specializes in Put-in-Bay clothing created on the island.

BAY DESIGNS

(Delaware Ave., Across from Carriage House) Bay Designs' specialty is nautical gold and silver jewelry.

BLUE COTTAGE GALLERY

(185 Toledo Ave. ☎ 419.285.2128) Really more of an art gallery than just a "store," Blue Cottage showcases area artists who work in various mediums, such as oil painting, watercolor, jewelry, stained glass, ceramics, metal, and photography. Visitors can usually meet the artists and watch them at work on Saturdays. And if the artistic vibe rubs off on visitors, there are opportunities to attend classes. Blue Cottage also stocks CDs of the local entertainers.

CANDY BAR

(Delaware Ave. at the corner of Hartford Ave. ☎ 419.285.2920) Creator of Put-in-Bay's famous fudge, the Candy Bar is seldom missed by island visitors. Its fudge is 1/2 lb. a slice. The store is also popular for its children's novelty candy, saltwater taffy, and pretty much anything edible that can be dipped in chocolate including fresh fruit, pretzels, and cookies. Visitors cannot feel guilty for indulging; there's a rule on Put-in-Bay – you must leave all guilt shore side. There's no room for it on the island.

THE CARGO NET

(Langram Rd. ☎ 419.285.4231) Located about a block from **Miller Ferry's** dock, the Cargo Net accommodates visitors by private appointment only. It is worth the effort if one has an interest in nautical antiques and collectibles. Telephone ahead to arrange a private showing.

Bass Islands

CARRIAGE HOUSE

(Delaware Ave. ☎ 419.285.2212) This novelty shop has a little bit of everything, including children's items. It is fun to browse and has the tickets for **Kimberley's Carousel**.

COUNTRY HOUSE

(Delaware Ave. ☎ 419.285.3104) The Country House is one of the bigger stores in Put-in-Bay. Although not necessarily unique to the island, it truly has something for everyone, from babies to grandparents, and toddlers to college students. There are usually sale items on offer and weekly theme items to delight the imagination, including Christmas in July.

DEL SOL

(Harbor Village ☎ 419.285.1111
⚲ putinbay.com/advertisers/delsol/index.html) Everything sold at Del Sol changes color in the sunlight, including shirts, shorts, nail polish, jewelry, watches, toys, and polarized sun glasses (to name a few).

ISLAND SURF SHOP

(Catawba Ave.) The Surf Shop features a selection of summer clothing and accessories for men and women such as swim suits, shorts, dresses, bags, and shoes.

JESSIE'S JEWELRY

(Bay View Ave.) Located next to **Wharfside**, Jessie's Jewelry is a family business that specializes in handmade custom wire-wrapped jewelry. Visitors can browse island-theme items or order a special piece. There are also hand-painted scarves and purses from Bali to tempt one's imagination.

LAKESIDE OUTFITTERS

(Delaware Ave.) Men's and women's designer clothing and accessories can be found at Lakeside Outfitters. Some tee-shirts are sold in sizes up to 6X.

LOONEY BIN

(Catawba Ave.) Turn your sense of humor loose in the Looney Bin and start looking for novelty items, strange and silly. Also, island wine favorites are sold here at the state minimum from the local wineries.

MARINERS LOCKER

(Hartford Ave. ☎ 419.285.7005) Mariners Locker sells upscale clothes and accessories for men.

MISTY BAY BOUTIQUE

(Delaware Ave. ☎ 419.285.7005) Misty Bay has clothing and accessories for men, women, and children.

OH-MI GOODNESS

(Catawba Ave. ☎ 419.285.2405) This shop takes off on the Ohio State/Michigan rivalry with entertaining gifts and clothing.

PUDDLE DUCK SHOP

(Hartford Ave. ☎ 419.285.3200) This shop offers clothing for men and women.

PUT-IN-BAY T-SHIRT SHOP

(Hartford Ave. ☎ 419.285.7006) This is the place to find a Put-in-Bay souvenir tee-shirt or other souvenirs. The shop stays open late on Friday and Saturday.

Bass Islands

SILLY GOOSE

(Catawba Ave.) Silly Goose frequently generates exclamations of delight from first-time visitors as they discover the many and varied quality items for sale, ranging from local artwork to baby clothes, to the ever popular Wake Up Crabby Bloody Mary Mix. There are also Put-in-Bay sweatshirts and Robeez slipper shoes – just to name a few of the oohs and aahs to be found among the treasures waiting to be discovered.

WHARFSIDE

(Bay View Ave., Next to the Boardwalk ☎ 419.285.4511)
Wharfside, on the water, is stocked with all the marine supplies you will surely need while on the island, including fishing licenses and live bait, pots and pans, maps, and gifts. The shop even freezes all those fish that will eventually be caught. Also available are fresh coffee, cold drinks, and breakfast sandwiches. If you need something and it is not on display, just ask – they may just have it.

DINING

From seafood to pizzas and some delicious local cuisine, Put-in-Bay offers enough dining options to please every palate.

THE BOARDWALK BOOK'S SEAFOOD AND THE UPPER DECK

(Bay View Ave. ☎ 419.285.5665 🖱 the-boardwalk.com) Seafood and fresh fish, especially the lobster bisque and fresh lake perch, make for an enjoyable meal. Tableside service is included on the Upper Deck as is musical entertainment. There is also full bar service.

CAMEO PIZZA

(Catawba Ave. ☎ 419.285.4444 🖱 cameopizza.com) Part of a family operation, Cameo Pizza has been serving the public its own secret recipe since 1936.

CHICKEN PATIO

(Delaware Ave. ☎ 419.285.3581) The Chicken Patio is easy to find; follow the savory smell. The restaurant is famous for its homemade BBQ sauce, made fresh daily. Patrons can watch the chicken cooking on the 21-foot charcoal grill and enjoy the results with corn on the cob, potato salad, and dinner roll.

CRESCENT TAVERN

(Delaware Ave. ☎ 419.285.4211) Next to the **Chicken Patio** is the charming Victorian era Crescent Tavern, whose antique bar in the Tap Room alone is worth seeing. Good food and service is a staple at the Crescent. Its prime rib is not to be missed.

THE GOAT SOUP AND WHISKEY

(820 Catawba Ave. ☎ 419.285.GOAT) Take Catawba Avenue out from downtown toward **Heineman's Winery** and you will find the "Goat" on the way. It will be difficult to decide whether it is the location or the food that is the best feature. Soups are the specialty here, made fresh daily, so do not hesitate to ask the wait person for recommendations. The location originally was a winery; it makes for a pretty and peaceful stop on your island sightseeing.

MOSSBACK'S ISLAND BAR & GRILLE

(Corner of Catawba and Bay View ☎ 419.285.8888) Mossback's offers a full menu, but specializes in fresh lake perch and

Bass Islands

walleye. Lunch and dinner is served every day, including children's menu; breakfast is served on the weekends.

PRESS HOUSE JOE'S BAR

(Catawba Ave., Red Barn at the end ☎ 419.285.2716) Joe's Bar's Motto is, "Beer is Food. Eat at Joe's." One can have cocktails and beer here, or buy takeout. Another option is one of Joe's signature sandwiches, such as his Sloppy Scottie. Prices are reasonable. The atmosphere is casual and local. It also serves as a beverage store.

PUT-IN-BAY BREWING CO

(441 Catawba Ave. ☎ 419.285.4677 ☗ putinbaybrewery.com) Enjoy your sandwiches and fries with freshly brewed beer at this pub. The upper level has a DJ providing musical entertainment and two full-service bars. There is a dance club at night, which stays open until 2:30 a.m.

ROUNDHOUSE

(Delaware Ave. ☎ 419.285.2525 ☗ theroundhousebar.com) Good music, good friends, and good beer – what could be a better tradition? This is the point of view at Roundhouse anyway. People have been having a good time here since 1873. Whether one comes for the famous bucket of beer or just to people-watch, eat peanuts, and listen to the music, it takes work to not have fun at the Roundhouse. Check the Web site for times and music gigs.

THE SKYWAY RESTAURANT & LOUNGE

(Langram Rd. ☎ 419.285.4331 ☗ put-in-bayskyway.com) The Skyway offers special menus which can be viewed online and it also has a catering service. It often hosts theme dinners and is open year round. Check out the Martini Menu as well.

MIDDLE BASS ISLAND

On your trip to South Bass Islands, be sure to drop by Middle Bass as well. It may not have as many things to do and places to explore as South Bass, but is definitely worth a stopover. Middle Bass Island is not completely devoid of entertainment, but it has no intention of competing with Put-in-Bay for partying. In addition to the one at St. Hazards there is **J.F. Walleyes Eatery and Brewery,** a microbrewery and restaurant with full menu where "the good times roll." There is also a **General Store** and a **gift shop**. Middle Bass Island offers a quiet venue for a relaxed getaway vacation. There are a few lodging choices on the island.

MIDDLE BASS ISLAND INN

(🖱 **middlebassinn.com**) This historic red-brick inn sits on a secluded dead-end street near the beach. It is a favored venue for weddings and vacationers seeking a beach with peace and quiet.

ST. HAZARDS WATERFRONT RESORT

(🖱 **sthazards.com**) St. Hazards is set up as a village selection of condos, cabins, and villa rentals plus camping options and a microbrewery too. Accommodation options, rates, and reservation conditions are explained on the Web site.

Bass Islands

The deep glacial grooves discovered on Kelleys Island are believed to be among the largest exposed grooves in the world.

Kelleys Island

Kelleys Island is the largest of the U.S. western islands of Lake Erie. In the context of the United States history, Kelleys Island was part of the Connecticut land grant for the Western Reserve, like Sandusky. Prior to that it belonged to the Native Americans, the glaciers, and the dinosaurs.

AREA HISTORY

Deep glacial grooves discovered on Kelleys Island long ago attest to the power and presence of the receding glacier of the ending Ice Age. They are believed to be among the largest exposed grooves in the world, if not "the" largest. The glacier that carved these grooves is known as the Wisconsin Glacier. A walking tour of the grooves is a popular tourist activity on Kelleys Island and for local residents as well.

Historians are fairly certain that the Erie Indians lived on Kelleys Island until they were run out by the Iroquois tribe circa 1665. **Inscription Rock,** located on the south side of Kelleys Island, is inscribed with petroglyphs believed to have been carved by the Eries to record their history during their time there.

Kelleys Island's first European settler is said to have been a man named Cunningham who arrived around 1800. In 1817, the island became part of the Connecticut Land Company, which divided it into 13 parcels. Eventually, two brothers from Cleveland named Kelley, acquired all these parcels in the 1830s and began to encourage development of the island. Like the land on South Bass Island and around Sandusky, Kelleys, as the island became named, proved to be a good prospect for grape growing for wine, rock quarrying, fruit growing, and, of course, fishing. Life in the early 1800s for the new settlers in Sandusky and the Lake Erie Islands must have seemed like the Promised Land.

Fishing has always been a Great Lakes passion, no less so at Kelleys Island. Fish stories abound for as long as memory serves. Fishing, hunting, wine making, limestone quarrying – these main industries were sources of commerce for the big island nine miles out from Sandusky. Kelleys Island did not have a Cedar Point to draw in tourism, but even in the 19th century, its promise of providing such a haven was well recognized, and those who could afford it looked to the island for summer homes and private escape. The *Sandusky Register*, on August 28, 1873, described Kelleys Island thus:

> *"Kelleys Island is admirably adapted for recreation and amusement. The health inspiring and balmy breezes, the grand natural facilities for rational enjoyment, the superior opportunities to observe and study the sublimities of nature, … all conduce to make Kelleys island better suited to quietude and rest from the cares of the ordinary routine of business life than any existing similar resort….*
>
> *Commercially Kelleys Island is eminently superior to any other in Erie's Archipelago and had her early settlers invested their capital in the erection of magnificent hotels… she would have stood to-day a formidable rival of Cape May, Saratoga or Long Branch."*

Kelleys Island today has achieved a remarkable resolution of the dichotomy described in the 1873 musings of the local newspaper. It has preserved its lands from utter commercial destruction through its park and wildlife preservation efforts. At the same time it has capitalized its "health inspiring and balmy breezes" for tourism, but not in a manner that has overrun it into ruination. In a world where such a thing is next to impossible to achieve, Kelleys Island has kept its identity and made it its capital.

GETTING AROUND

People access Kelleys Island by their own boats, by plane, or ferry (using the latter to bring personal cars or RVs). Having settled in, all that is really needed to get around is a more simple means of locomotion. Bicycles and golf carts are ideal.

GOLF CART RENTALS

(☎ 419.746.2808) Without a doubt, one of the best ways to get around Kelleys Island is by golf cart – unless one prefers horseback or bicycle. Many people often ferry their horses over in their trailers for a ride for the day or a camping weekend.

THINGS TO DO

Even with its laidback atmosphere, people will find several things to keep themselves occupied at Kelleys Island, including fishing or simply walking around soaking up island life.

CAPTAIN PARK'S FISHING CHARTER

(Park Schafer, Seaway Marina ☎ 888.306.7835/419.656.9908/ 419.433.4536 🖥 captainpark.com) Fishing is a serious pursuit off Kelleys Island. Captain Park's Fishing Charter operates on the island to assist visitors. Children are welcome. More detailed information is available on the Web site.

KELLEYS ISLAND STATE PARK

(☎ 419.746.2546) From the Kelleys Island Ferry, go west on Lakeshore Drive, turn right on Division Street and follow it to the end. The State Park is on the right and occupies a fair section of the island. It offers year-round activities, although some of the camping amenities are seasonal. Both electric and non-electric campsites are available as well as boat-launching ramps, a swimming beach, hiking trails, kayak rentals, hunting and fishing (limits and licensed), summertime nature and youth programs, and picnic facilities. Winter opportunities include ice fishing, ice skating, and cross-country skiing. Most of the camping sites can be reserved. Call ahead for details about specific activities that are available for visiting only for a specific time.

CHARLES HERNDON GALLERIES

(☎ 419.746.2249 🖱 charlesherndon.com) When artist Charles Herndon retired from teaching at the Columbus College of Art and Design, he returned to Kelleys Island, a fondly remembered place of his youth. Now an artist in residence, he creates sculptured beauty from the natural stone of the island. Painting and photography also grace his studio. It is best to call ahead to be sure the gallery will be open for a specific visit.

WALKING AROUND THE GLACIAL GROOVES AND HIKING AND CYCLING THE ISLAND

Some of the best fun on the island costs no more than the cost of getting there. The beauty of hiking or bicycling along the beach road and through the state park, studying the glacial grooves, and Native American petroglyphs, pausing for a picnic and bird-watching, or simply resting in the shade, Kelleys Island is a haven for nature lovers.

ACCOMMODATIONS

Kelleys Island is primarily residential. It is not the shopping center that one finds on Put-in-Bay. There are places to eat, drink, and be merry, and many places to tour and stay. There are also marinas and serious fishing arrangements that can be made with advance planning. A large portion of the island however, is privately residential and a significant portion is state park. The ambience is relaxed, fun, and everything operates at a slower pace. Kelleys Island is charming and peaceful and intends to stay that way. It is why people come here. It is why people live here.

Debarking the car ferry from Marblehead, a left turn on Lakeshore Drive will take the visitor to the village center on Kelleys Island. Lakeshore Drive winds around the edge of the island, providing a stunning view and access to most of the B&Bs and hotels. In-island has more places to stay and campgrounds, as well as the airstrip and private residences, some of which are for rent on a limited basis during the summer season through private arrangements and word-of-mouth. There are also year-round island dwellers, who would have it no other way.

CAMPBELL COTTAGE B&B

(932 W. Lakeshore Dr. ☎ 877.746.2740 ⬯ campbellcottage.com)
Three pleasant air-conditioned rooms with their own baths provide privacy and an old-fashioned front porch provides a lake view at the Campbell Cottage B&B. A full breakfast is served and additional amenities include renting bicycles. Snacks and coffee, iced tea, or lemonade are offered to guests all day. When reservations are made, the Campbells send out a welcome package to assist a smooth and easy arrival.

EAGLE'S NEST B&B

(216 Cameron Rd. ☎ eaglesnestbnb.com) Three air-conditioned suites with full breakfast come with the Eagle's Nest B&B. Children are welcome. Rooms and grounds can be viewed on the Web site.

A WATER'S EDGE RETREAT

(827 E. Lakeshore Dr. ☎ 419.746.2333/800.884.5143) This highly rated, three-story, colorful luxury bed and breakfast is located right on the water and provides a unique sanctuary from life's stresses. Six rooms are available. Package deals can include a sail on the owners' 35-foot yacht and use of their golf cart. Breakfast is a gourmet treat.

HOUSE ON HUNTINGTON LANE

(117 Huntington Lane ☎ houseonhuntington.com) This house offers a bed and continental breakfast arrangement with a minimum two nights on weekend stays. The restored century home has wireless Internet and direct TV in its air-conditioned rooms, which are equipped with their own baths. Bicycles are provided for guests' use. Ask about off-season rates and the cancellation policy.

CRICKET LODGE

(111 E. Lakeshore Dr. ☎ cricketlodge.com) Once the summer home of successful vaudevillians, Cricket Lodge now happily plays to its own private audience of guests for bed and breakfast. It provides four comfortably appointed bedrooms and a lovely common room and porch with a view.

THE INN ON KELLEYS ISLAND

(317 W. Lakeshore Dr. 🖰 kelleysisland.com/theinn) The Inn offers four charming rooms and shared baths in a century home with the prized Lakeshore view of the water. Photos and additional information are available on the Web site. There are certain pricing requirements and reservation restrictions.

MORNING GLORY INN

(135 Morning Glory Lane ☎ 419.746.2560) Complete privacy, comfort, and beauty are some of the special features of the Morning Glory Inn. It is situated on 15 acres and has its own beach. The rooms are decorated with antiques and the Country Garden Suite comes with its own bath and private entrance. Weekly or weekend rentals may be arranged as well. Call for additional information and reservations.

PASCOE HOUSE B&B

(111 Chapel St. ☎ 419.746.2705/419.656.6170) Pascoe House has two small rooms, each with its own full bath in a pleasant old frame house. One room has its own balcony.

SUNRISE POINT

(515 E. Lakeshore Dr. 🖰 sunrisepointKI.com) Sunrise Point is set up as four efficiency units, each with its own entrance. It is located on the water at the island's southeast side, with its own private dock and beach.

KELLEYS ISLAND FIRST CLASS CONDOS

(111 W. Lakeshore Dr. ☎ 419.271.1609
🖰 kelleysislandchamber.com) Three-bedroom, two-bath condos are available for rent by the week. Features include a heated

pool, washer/dryer, TV-DVD-VCR, and cooking utensils. Photos and additional information available on Web site. Be sure to check into special off-season rates.

MOONGLOW CONDO

(Quarry Condos, E. Lakeshore Dr.

🖱 **kelleysislandchamber.com/members/moonglowcondos.htm)**
This is a two-bedroom, two-bath air-conditioned unit available by the week or weekend. Features include a TV, outdoor grill, guest dock, and linens. It is reasonably priced and available year-round. Children are welcome but no pets.

SHOPPING

You can browse around the shops on the island to purchase some one-of-a-kind items to take back as souvenirs of your tip to Kelleys Island.

BROWNS GENERAL STORE

(☎ 419.746.2357) Staying on the island means shopping for various grocery items, newspapers, and sundry needs. Browns General Store fits the bill.

ORIGINAL ISLAND FUDGE SHOPPE

(109 Division Dr.) Something about vacations and fudge go together, especially on the Lake Erie Islands. Every vacation spot seems to have a fudge shop and Kelleys Island's home-made Fudge Shoppe is first rate. It is accompanied by a selection of fountain drinks and ice cream too.

UNEEK CARGO SHOP

(633 W. Lakeshore Dr.) Uneek offers an eclectic selection of gift items, from furniture to body lotions.

VI'S ISLAND TREASURES

(125 Division St.) VI'S Island Treasures is a retail shop that sells a variety of upscale items such as Swarovski crystal sunglasses, clothing, and 14-karat gold and sterling silver jewelry, including SoFo, the custom-designed fused glass jewelry of Cheryl and John Soforia. SoFo jewelry is also featured at **Firelands Gift Shop** *(1101 Decatur St.)* in Sandusky.

WACKY SHACK

(633 W. Lakeshore Dr.) As the name suggests, all things wacky are sold at Wacky Shack. This is a novelty shop for fun and party items, like Mardi Gras beads, hats, and glow sticks, to name a few of the usual but perennially fun stuff.

RESTAURANTS

There are several restaurants to choose from to enjoy a tasty meal and wonderful views. Recommended below are some choice restaurants where visitors to the island will relish dining.

BAG THE MOON SALOON

(No. 109 on Lakeshore Dr. ☎ 419.746.2365
🖰 **kelleysislandchamber.com/members/bagthemoon.htm)** Keep in mind that "downtown" at Kelleys Island is not much more than a block or two. So most places are not hard to find. Bag the Moon is on the main Lakeshore Drive across the street from the water. It is a family restaurant, not too big, casual, and

wonderful. Breakfast is recommended and comes as a welcome sight after a late night of partying, or any night for that matter. The restaurant runs daily specials such as steak night, taco night, and boneless chicken wings all day. The food is good, the service is friendly, and the prices are reasonable. Nighttime entertainment is lively because, after all, this is a "party tavern." Weekends have live entertainment. Remember to ask about the strawberry shot. Call or check the Web site for the party schedule and daily specials. Most people have a good time just stopping in and taking pot luck.

THE CASINO RESTAURANT & MARINA
(104 Division Dr. ☎ 419.746.2773 🖢 kelleysislandcasino.com) The Casino is one of the island's favorite watering holes. With its transient dockage, boaters are fond of pulling in for dinner and drinks and an evening of entertainment. Live entertainment is featured on Saturday afternoons in the summer season; the best entertainment of all, however, is the view of the water and people-watching, for the Casino is a lively place. The *Jet Express* and the *Goodtime* pick up and drop off their passengers at the Casino dock.

THE VILLAGE PUMP
(103 Lakeshore Dr. ☎ 419.746.2281) No trip to Kelleys Island could be complete without a visit to The Village Pump. The fresh Lake Erie perch alone – sandwich or dinner – is worth the trip to Kelleys Island and is an island tradition. If perch is not one's preference, there is the sumptuous Pump Burger, lobster chowder, and other worthwhile menu choices. Full bar service is available, as well as pool tables and wireless high-speed Internet (not an easy find on the island).

KELLEYS ISLAND WINE CO.

(420 Woodford Rd. ☎ 419.746.2678 🖥 kelleysislandwine.com)
This is the island's only winery and it makes the most of it
with wine tasting, a winery-viewing room, full restaurant, and
outdoor area for picnicking and strolling to enjoy the grounds.
There is a children's play area and rumor has it one might be
able to get up a game of horse shoes. The restaurant fare in
the afternoon is limited to hors d'oeuvres-styled platters of
domestic and imported cheeses served with French bread,
fresh fruit, and the special house mustard; meat and fish with
stuffed olives and hummus; combination platters; and creative
pizzas. In the evening, the restaurant expands its menu to
full dinners featuring the fresh catch of the day, shrimp, Thai
chicken, or strip steak on skewers, pasta, salads of fresh greens,
and tiramisu and special desserts of the day.

CAPTAIN'S CORNER

(101 Lakeshore Dr., Corner of Division St. ☎ 419.746.2112)
Captain's Corner features Mediterranean and Greek menu
selections, as well as steak, tuna, and sushi plus specialty
desserts to tempt the palate. It also features full bar service and
John Christ wine made in Avon Lake, Ohio.

KELLEYS ISLAND BREWERY

(504 W. Lakeshore Dr. ☎ 419.746.2314/419.746.2820) Located
on Kelleys Island's south shore, the Kelleys Island Brewery
sells homemade beer along with a menu of pub fare for breakfast, lunch, and dinner. Beer selections include ales, seasonal
beers, and root beer, all brewed on-site. Wine and cocktails are
also available. The regular season is May through November,
and its peak summer season hours are 7:30 a.m. to 11:30 p.m.

Kelleys Island

Call to confirm hours during spring and fall, and to find out the days that the brewery may be closed. Currently, it is not open to the public in the winter season.

P F DOCKERS

(114 W. Lakeside Dr. ☎ 419.746.2100) Here is a great find facing Portside Marina. A flat screen TV is up for sports fans and prices are reasonable for good food. Try the Fettucine Alfredo or the ribeye steak sandwich. For breakfast lovers, P F Dockers is perfect for your sunrise breakfast.

About the Author

Linda Clark Ashar is a fourth generation resident of Vermilion in Erie County, Ohio. A lawyer, educator, freelance writer, artist, and amateur photographer, Linda is a dedicated world traveler and observer of people and cultures. Linda lives at Thornapple Farms with her husband Mike, also a lawyer, where they raise Morgan horses and rare Irish Kerry Bog Ponies.

Index

Index

Index

NOTES:

NOTES:

NOTES:

NOTES:

NOTES:

NOTES:

⌐✫tourist town guides®

Explore America's Fun Places

Books in the *Tourist Town Guides*® series are available at bookstores and online. You can also visit our Web site for additional book and travel information. The address is:

http://www.touristtown.com

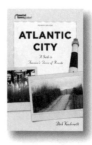

Atlantic City (4th Edition)

This guide will introduce a new facet of Atlantic City that goes beyond the appeal exercised by its lavish casinos. Atlantic City is one of the most popular vacation destinations in the United States.

Price: $14.95; ISBN: 978-1-935455-00-4

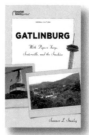

Gatlinburg (2nd Edition)

Whether it is to see the weird and wonderful displays at Ripley's Believe It or Not! Museum, or to get the adrenaline pumping with some outdoor activity or to revel in the extravaganza of Dollywood, people come to the Smokies for a variety of reasons – and they are never disappointed!

Price: $14.95; ISBN: 978-1-935455-04-2

Hilton Head

A barrier island off the coast of South Carolina, Hilton Head is a veritable coastal paradise. This destination guide gives a detailed account of this resort island, tailor made for a coastal vacation.

Price: $14.95; ISBN: 978-1-935455-06-6

Myrtle Beach (2nd Edition)

The sunsets are golden and the pace is relaxed at Myrtle Beach, the beachside playground for vacationers looking for their fill of sun, sand, and surf. Head here for the pristine beaches, the shopping opportunities, the sea of attractions, or simply to kick back and unwind.

Price: $14.95; ISBN: 978-1-935455-01-1

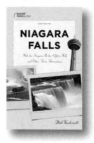

Niagara Falls (3rd Edition)

The spirited descent of the gushing falls may be the lure for you, but in Niagara Falls, it is the smorgasbord of activities and attractions that will keep you coming back for more!

Price: $14.95; ISBN: 978-1-935455-03-5

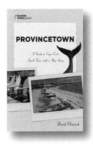

Provincetown

With a rich heritage and proud history, Provincetown is America's oldest art colony, but there is more to this place than its culture. The guide to Provincetown explores its attractions and accommodations, culture and recreation in detail to reveal a vacation destination definitely worth exploring.

Price: $13.95; ISBN: 978-1-935455-07-3

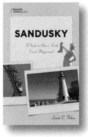

Sandusky

The Cedar Point Amusement Park may be the main reason to visit Sandusky, but this comprehensive guide provides ample reason to stick around and explore the area and the neighboring islands.

Price: $13.95; ISBN: 978-0-9767064-5-8

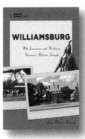

Williamsburg

The lure to explore history is unmistakable in the town, but Williamsburg is so much more than its rich history. Head to this region to discover the modern facets of this quaint town, indulge in activities guaranteed to hook your interest, and step into the past in this historically significant destination.

Price: $14.95; ISBN: 978-1-935455-05-9

Also Available: (See http://www. touristtown.com for details)

Black Hills	Price: $14.95; ISBN: 978-0-9792043-1-9)
Breckenridge	Price: $14.95; ISBN: 978-0-9767064-9-6)
Frankenmuth	Price: $13.95; ISBN: 978-0-9767064-8-9)
Hershey	Price: $13.95; ISBN: 978-0-9792043-8-8)
Jackson Hole	Price: $14.95; ISBN: 978-0-9792043-3-3)
Key West (2nd Edition)	Price: $14.95; ISBN: 978-1-935455-02-8)
Las Vegas	Price: $14.95; ISBN: 978-0-9792043-5-7)
Mackinac	Price: $14.95; ISBN: 978-0-9767064-7-2)
Ocean City	Price: $13.95; ISBN: 978-0-9767064-6-5)
Wisconsin Dells	Price: $13.95; ISBN: 978-0-9792043-9-5)

www.touristtown.com

ORDER FORM #1
ON REVERSE SIDE

Tourist Town Guides® is published by:
Channel Lake, Inc.
P.O. Box 1771
New York, NY 10156

ORDER FORM

Telephone: With your credit card handy,
call toll-free 800.592.1566

Fax: Send this form toll-free to 866.794.5507

E-mail: Send the information on this form
to orders@channellake.com

Postal mail: Send this form with payment to Channel Lake, Inc.
P.O. Box 1771, New York, NY, 10156

Your Information: ( ) Do not add me to your mailing list

Name: _____

Address: _____

City: _____ State: _____ Zip: _____

Telephone: _____

E-mail: _____

Book Title(s) / ISBN(s) / Quantity / Price
(see previous page or www.touristtown.com for this information)

_____

_____

_____

Total payment*: $_____

Payment Information: (Circle One)   Visa / Mastercard

Number: _____ Exp: _____

Or, make check payable to: **Channel Lake, Inc.**

** Add the lesser of $6.50 USD or 18% of the total purchase price
for shipping. International orders call or e-mail first! New York
orders add 8% sales tax.*

www.touristtown.com

ORDER FORM #2
ON REVERSE SIDE

Tourist Town Guides® is published by:
Channel Lake, Inc.
P.O. Box 1771
New York, NY 10156

ORDER FORM

Telephone: With your credit card handy, call toll-free 800.592.1566

Fax: Send this form toll-free to 866.794.5507

E-mail: Send the information on this form to orders@channellake.com

Postal mail: Send this form with payment to Channel Lake, Inc. P.O. Box 1771, New York, NY, 10156

Your Information: ( ) Do not add me to your mailing list

Name: _____

Address: _____

City: _____ State: _____ Zip: _____

Telephone: _____

E-mail: _____

Book Title(s) / ISBN(s) / Quantity / Price
(see previous page or www.touristtown.com for this information)

_____

_____

_____

Total payment*: $_____

Payment Information: (Circle One)   Visa / Mastercard

Number: _____ Exp: _____

Or, make check payable to: **Channel Lake, Inc.**

* Add the lesser of $6.50 USD or 18% of the total purchase price for shipping. International orders call or e-mail first! New York orders add 8% sales tax.